living with less

——— so your ———

family has more

living with less

less

so your

family has

more

BY JILL SAVAGE
AND MARK SAVAGE

Guideposts

Living with Less, So Your Family Has More

ISBN-13: 978-0-8249-4801-6

Published by Guideposts
16 East 34th Street
New York, New York 10016
www.guideposts.com

Distributed by Ideals Publications, a division of Guideposts
2636 Elm Hill Pike, Suite 120
Nashville, Tennessee 37214

Guideposts and *Ideals* are registered trademarks of Guideposts.

Acknowledgments
Scripture quotations marked (THE MESSAGE) are taken from *The Message.*
Copyright © 1993, 1994, 1995, 1996, 2000, 2001, 2002 by Eugene H. Peterson.

Scripture quotations marked (NIV) are taken from *The Holy Bible, New International Version.* Copyright © 1973, 1978, 1984 International Bible Society. Used by permission of Zondervan Bible Publishers.

Scripture quotations marked (NLT) are taken from the *Holy Bible*, New Living Translation. Copyright © 1996. Used by permission of Tyndale House Publishers, Inc., Wheaton, Illinois 60189. All rights reserved.

Library of Congress Cataloging-in-Publication Data

Savage, Jill.
    Living with less: so your family has more / by Jill Savage and Mark Savage.
    p. cm.
    ISBN 978-0-8249-4801-6
    1. Finance, Personal. 2. Contentment. 3. Families.
    4. Thriftiness. I. Savage, Jill, 1964- II. Title.
    HG179.S23955 2010
    332.024–dc22   2009051568

Cover by Mingovits Design
Interior design by Lorie Pagnozzi
Typeset by Aptara

Printed and bound in the United States of America
10 9 8 7 6 5 4 3 2 1

contents

acknowledgments

THIS BOOK HAS BEEN A HUGE COLLABORATIVE EFFORT! Not only is it the first book we've written together, but it was also conceived out of hundreds of conversations with wonderful families who have shared their hearts with us over the years. With that in mind, we'd like to offer special thanks to:

- Our prayer partners, who have prayed over these words and the entire process of writing. Special thanks to Becky for your fabulous communication with the prayer team.
- Our manuscript readers Brenda, Lisa, MarLo, Michael, Megan, Becky, Crystal, Tyler, Dave and Dustin. Thank you for taking the time to read and give us valuable feedback. You were willing to ask the tough questions and help shape and form this important resource for families.
- The Hearts at Home team. Your vision to encourage the family is greatly needed in this world.
- Our two Beths: Beth Jusino, our Alive Communications literary agent, and Beth Adams, our Guideposts editor. And we can't forget Andrea Heinecke, who stepped in midway through the process to continue representing us through Alive after God took Beth Jusino into a new field. Thank you all for believing in the message of this book. It's been a pleasure working with all of you.

- Our incredible family. Thanks, kids, for being willing to make dinner, clean up the kitchen, and do a few more loads of laundry than you usually do. You've been encouraging, patient and very helpful. Erica, we proved that you can write a book and plan a wedding at the same time!
- Our Savior, Jesus Christ. You've changed our hearts and opened our eyes to the "more" in life. Thank you for your grace, your hope and your truth, which continue to transform our lives.

foreword

I COULDN'T RESIST...

When I'm asked to write forewords to books, I routinely turn those requests down. But this time, I couldn't resist. Jill Savage is not only a great lady, but she also heads a wonderful organization, Hearts at Home, that I believe heartily in. Hearts at Home ministers to moms—the ones I call "the warriors of the home." These talented and determined women, who could leap skyscrapers in a single bound, are what makes the world go round for everyone in the family. What would we do without them?

In *Living With Less So Your Family Has More,* Jill and Mark Savage have focused on what's most important to family life. Our culture believes that, in general, bigger is better, and the ones with the most toys win. But that's simply not true. Our kids don't need the best houses, the best cars, the best clothes, and they certainly don't need to be run from door to door like little gerbils on a wheel. What they need is time with their parents—the best mom and the best dad that less stress and fewer activities can buy. But how can we live like this in today's frenzied world?

Living with less materially actually can provide more relationally, allowing us to experience more time with those who matter most as well as more peace in our hearts and minds. After all, in the long run, what's more important—that you run from activity to activity, making sure you check everything off the "to do" list on your Black-Berry, or that you have more time to invest in your marriage and your children?

To live the less-is-more life, the Savages say that a husband and wife need to address three important areas. First, what vision do you have for your family? What do you want your family life to look like? Second, what attitudes do you need to adopt to successfully live this out? And third, what actions do you need to take as a family to simplify your life? Specifically, are there ways you could live on less money to allow you more time for what's really important?

This book is designed for husbands and wives to read *together*. No Lone Ranger stuff here, but a workable plan and a unified vision of keeping family first.

Living with Less So Your Family Has More is about living life intentionally *today*, so that you can live without regret *tomorrow*. I highly recommend it.

Dr. Kevin Leman
Author of *Have a New Kid by Friday* and
Have a New Husband by Friday

introduction ─────────────────

HAVE YOU WANTED TO GIVE YOUR FAMILY MORE BUT YOU'RE NOT QUITE SURE WHAT "MORE" REALLY MEANS? Maybe that's why you picked up this book. It could be that you're searching for something. It could be that there's something unsettled inside you.

Or maybe it's the "less" that caught your eye. Less stress. Less work. Less anxiety. Less tension. Perhaps you simply long to get off the treadmill of life and really start living.

We've had those very same thoughts ourselves. And we decided to do something about it. We've chosen to live with less money, less activity and less stress. In a world that says that "bigger is better," we've chosen to believe that "less is really more." And we've realized that we're living the "more" that we were looking for all along.

When we're pedaling as fast as we can financially, it's all too easy to miss the unique season we're in while raising a family. The opportunities to influence our children, enjoy our family and invest in these relationships present themselves just once in life. You can't go back and parent again. We've experienced this personally over the past four years as three of our five children have married and established families and homes of their own. For the most part, we've been able to look back on the past twenty-five years of parenting with little regret.

But unfortunately that's not the experience of many families. We've had the unique opportunity to mentor other couples over the years. We've seen far too many looking back and regretting the decisions they made: taking on too much debt; working so hard to provide financially for the family that they now realize they don't really know their kids like they want to; or being involved in so many activities outside of the home that their spouse and children resented those commitments.

Our hope is to save families from these kinds of regrets. When we think through our years of helping other families, we have noted that much of the regret is centered around believing that more is better: more money, more career, more activities. In buying that lie, parents have gone deeper in debt trying to provide material things their kids really don't need, alienated their children while serving the community, compromised their marriage by living on a crazy schedule packed with activities, and stressed out their kids while providing them every opportunity possible. Is this really what we want for our families? We've found that more is not always better. In fact, we've found that when it comes to family life, less can actually be more!

This book will show you that it can be done. We're not financial experts, but we will talk about money. We're not marriage counselors, but we will help you talk with your spouse. We don't have all the answers, but we're excited to share with you the answers we have found. We believe they have the ability to be life-changing for you and your family. And we believe that enough to have let our own children eat way too many frozen pizzas for a period of time just to get this message in book form to share with you!

This book is a Hearts at Home resource. Hearts at Home (www.hearts-at-home.org) is an organization that encourages, educates and equips women in every stage of motherhood. God is using the Hearts at Home conferences, Web site, radio program and books to change families, one mom at a time. But this isn't just a book for moms. It's a book for both moms and dads. In fact, this is the first Hearts at Home resource written by a couple for couples. We believe that living with less so your family can have more is something that a married couple needs to explore together. And if you're a single parent who has picked up this book, don't put it down just yet. There's plenty for you to consider as well. In fact, you may just find that your less can actually be more in so many ways.

If you are reading this book as a couple, you may want to pick up some highlighters. If you choose to do that, Dad can use a blue highlighter and Mom can use a pink one. After you've both read a chapter and highlighted what you feel is important, take some time to talk about what you've read. See just how much purple you've created (probably not much if you're anything like us!). Look at where you've found the same things important. Talk about the places that are just pink and just blue and why you felt they were valuable points. If you'd like to go a step further, you can pray together about your developing vision for your family. If that's a new experience for you, just hold hands and talk with God together about your fears, hopes and dreams. Even with just a couple of sentences prayed together, you will take your marriage relationship to a deeper level of intimacy.

We've had many eyes look at this book as it has developed. One honest reader said, "This stuff is good to think about, but how do we even begin to talk about it as a couple?" That's why we've included a section called "Let's Talk About It" at the end of every chapter. If you're reading together, use the questions provided to get the conversation going. And if you're reading alone, you can use the section to ask yourself questions that will help you set your own strategies for giving your family more.

We want to get you thinking—to help you identify places where there is excess in your family that can be trimmed in exchange for better relationships. From experience, we have found that successfully living with less requires vision, attitudes and actions. Because of this, we have divided this book into three parts. Part One will define "less" and redefine "more." This will help clarify the vision that less can really be more, and will help you define a vision for your own family. Part Two will address the attitudes necessary to live with less. Some of these attitudes will be countercultural. They'll involve finding simplicity, sacrificing willingly, embracing frugality, and fostering faith. This section will help ready your heart for whatever changes you choose to make. Part Three will identify actions you can take to carry out your new vision and attitude. These proven strategies, gleaned from families who have learned to live with less, will equip you with practical ways your family can learn to live on less—and even like it!

Are you ready to figure out what this might look like for your family? Turn the page and start highlighting.

part 1: vision

**JILL REMEMBERS ONE PARTICULARLY CHALLENG-
ING DAY AS A PARENT.** Our youngest was a preschooler, and he had no desire to pick up his toys. She wanted him
to be responsible for cleaning up the mess he had made. He was
challenging her authority like never before. Going toe to toe with
a two-year-old was not on her list of things to do that day, and she
was both tired and tempted to just let it go.

But then she pictured this little one of ours as not so little anymore. Her imagination took her to a twenty-two-year-old arguing
with his boss at his first full-time job. She realized that was a recipe
for disaster, and there was something she could do about it right
then. She could establish her authority and help our son know that
rules are in place for a reason. They are not negotiable.

She decided this *was* a hill worth dying on and it was a battle she had to win. She realized that what she did that day would
affect his future. She was able to muster the strength and courage
to stand strong.

Ah...the power of vision.

THE POWER OF VISION

Living on less so your family can have more is a countercultural concept. If you're going to choose to live counterculturally, you'll need vision to stay on course for the long haul. The author Robert Collier said that vision "reaches beyond the thing that is, into the conception of what can be. Imagination gives you the picture. Vision gives you the impulse to make the picture your own." Those words are powerful for parents. We are the visionaries of the family. We have to have one eye on what is and one eye on what can be. In fact, if we don't, we'll find ourselves mired in the day-to-day challenges of living with less—and we'll likely burn out and risk apathy. We have to know where we want to go or we'll never have any chance of arriving there.

Several years ago in my book *Professionalizing Motherhood*, I challenged moms to reframe the concept of accomplishment. Moms—particularly stay-at-home moms—often find themselves wondering at the end of the day what exactly they had accomplished. My encouragement to them was to redefine their daily tasks in light of their long-term goals. When you can move from being near-sighted to being farsighted, you're able to see things with a different perspective. And farsightedness—that long-term vision—is desperately needed in parenthood. What we do today as parents will affect our children's tomorrow!

Too many of us live for the moment. Honestly, that's the way our culture is designed. Instant gratification far outweighs delayed gratification any day. We want what we want *now*, not later. But raising a family doesn't work that way. Forming the character of a young child into that of a mature adult takes time, energy, patience and tenacity. And when you're working at something for about eighteen years, having a vision of what you're working toward is of great importance.

What vision do you have for your family? Is the culture defining it? How about your circumstances? For example, do you see your children enjoying activities that are within reach financially and geographically? Do you long for a house full of laughter and creativity? Do you look down the road and see your children thriving in college and adulthood while you and your spouse reignite the fires at home? Is there a sense that less could actually result in more for your family?

Pastor and author Bill Hybels says that "vision leaks," and we've found that to be very true in our lives. When life gets busy, we can all forget why we're doing what we're doing. As we launch into the next chapter we'll cast a refreshing vision for families. And we'll discover that keeping our vision in front of us in as many ways as possible is very important to staying on track with what we *really* want for our family.

chapter 1

less is really more

"MOM, I CAN'T BELIEVE THE DIFFERENCE I FEEL WITH THIS NEW JOB," my daughter Anne said to me. "My house is clean for the first time in two years. My laundry is actually caught up and I went to lunch with a friend twice this week. I feel like I can breathe! I thought I would be upset about the paycheck, but it's like I've been given a new source of energy." This conversation happened just two weeks after Anne transitioned from a well-paid full-time job with a one-hour commute to a decent-paying part-time job just three miles from her house.

"You know, Anne," I said, trying to keep the grin off my face. "That's exactly why your dad and I have made so many of the choices we've made over the years. There are just some things in this world—like time—that money can't buy."

"I don't think I understood that until now," she said. "But it is so true."

That little interaction with our daughter proved to be the foundation for this book. Anne loved her job. She loved the money her job provided. She had a long commute in the Chicago area, but she felt that the generous salary she received made that worthwhile. But when the job disappeared compliments of a challenging economy, she suddenly found herself looking for new opportunities. Her new job came with a modest salary, but it was only five minutes from her house. She lost a chunk of her paycheck, but in the process, she gained more time. She found she was less stressed and more in control of her life.

For the first time, she found the money didn't matter as much as she thought it had. The extra time—which she could spend keeping her life in order and enjoying her husband and her friends—more than made up for the sacrifice.

Like Anne, we didn't always see these intangible benefits clearly, but most of us can feel when those things are absent. Maybe you've thought or even said aloud:

- I'm tired of living with constant stress.
- I feel disconnected from my spouse.
- I feel disconnected from my kids.
- I want to laugh again.
- I'm earning more but I feel like we're living with less.
- I'm tired of rushing from one activity to another.
- I'm weary of drive-thru meals.
- I just wish our family could sit around the dinner table each night laughing and talking about our day.
- I can't do this anymore: work, day care, soccer practice, quick meals and shallow relationships.
- There are not enough hours in the day.
- There has to be a simpler way of doing things.

If you have had those thoughts, you are not alone. We all want the best for our kids, but sometimes we lose sight of what "best" just might be. We want to give them more, but we've allowed the world to define our "more" as things that money can buy. We long to give them every opportunity possible, but we're missing out on being a family because there are just too many opportunities. We're focused on providing tangibles—things that money can buy—when what most of us really long for are intangibles—things that money can't buy. The pace of life that many of us are traveling at is actually hurting rather than helping our families.

You've obviously picked up this book for a reason. Maybe it's because you've said some of the statements above. Maybe your spouse has said some of the statements above and asked you to read this book together. Maybe you are looking for something different in your life, but you're just not sure what "different" might look like. Whatever the reason, we are glad you've chosen to explore the possibilities with us.

NO REGRETS

Even though we've been married nearly twenty-seven years, we began our less-is-more journey twenty-three years ago. After Jill finished her degree in music education at Butler University in Indianapolis, Indiana, we packed up our possessions and our young family and moved to Lincoln, Illinois. This move was meant to allow Mark to complete Bible college and make a career transition from sales to full-time ministry. We figured that Jill could work to support our family while Mark attended school and cared for the kids. We would only need day care for the kids while Mark attended classes.

Jill sent out dozens of résumés looking for a job teaching music in a school. There simply were no vacancies in any of the school districts within an hour of our new home. By necessity, we came up with a Plan B: We would do day care in our home as our primary source of income. Mark had the ability to install flooring, so he contributed to our income with part-time flooring jobs.

What happened over the next eighteen months ended up shaping our vision for our family. After caring for our own children and the day care children, both of us began to see that meeting a child's needs was not necessarily the same thing as providing for them financially. We witnessed the excitement of the older children when they jumped off the school bus and the stories of the day tumbled out of their mouths faster than we could grasp them. We captured precious moments as we snuggled, hugged, kissed boo-boos and read stories to the little ones throughout the day; we got to be a part of many of the most important moments in their days. By the time the moms and dads picked up their children, the excitement of the older children had disappeared and the little ones were fussy and ready for dinner and an early bedtime—and then they began the routine all over again the next morning. We realized that this wasn't how we wanted to live our lives. We wanted to be there for those moments in our own children's days.

A year and a half later, we made an unexpected move to Bloomington, Illinois, where I took a church internship. I finished my degree by commuting the thirty miles to Lincoln several times a week for the next two-and-a-half years. We determined that Jill would remain at home with our kids.

We pieced together a very meager income, with Jill still doing some day care and teaching private piano and voice lessons. I did part-time flooring jobs on the side. It was tight, but we were living out the beginning of our new vision for our family: one that included more snuggling and less running, more time and less money, more boundaries and less stress. It was during this period that we decided Jill would remain at home with the kids until they were in school. Once they were in school Jill could find a teaching job that would allow her to have summers off and similar school hours to the kids.'

This was a perfect plan ... except that we kept having children!

Just as one would get ready to enter kindergarten, the stick would turn blue. (And yes, we did know what was causing that.) But we soon made another discovery: As the older children entered their teen years, we expected them to need us less, but they actually needed us more. We adjusted our vision once again and determined that having one parent home with the kids until they were grown was valuable.

Today our five children range in age from thirteen to twenty-five. Anne (twenty-five) is married and lives with her husband Matt in northern Illinois. Evan (twenty-three) is married and lives in central Illinois with his wife Julie. Erica (nineteen) is married and lives with her husband Kendall wherever the Army takes them. Kolya (sixteen) is a freshman in high school. (Kolya is the newest addition to our family as we adopted him at the age of nine from an orphanage in Russia.) And Austin (thirteen) is an eighth-grader.

Over our years of marriage and raising a family, we've wrestled with so many questions along the way: What do we want to provide for our family? What do we *need* to provide for our family? What are the things we want for our family that money can't buy? Is it possible to live with less? What could we gain by simplifying schedules, increasing family time, or even adjusting career directions? What are the benefits of having one of us at home? What intangibles are so important that they warrant our consideration?

A dad has to wrestle with these questions in his own way. As a pastor raising five children, Mark certainly has. He wants so much for our family, but by society's standards he's limited in what he can provide. His income has never been much more than the American average. He has even struggled at times with feeling inadequate as a provider for our family because of the limited earning ability in his chosen career path. Learning to be okay with less has definitely been an adjustment for him.

A mom, too, has to consider these questions in a deeply personal way. Jill is a music teacher by trade, but she's been committed to the profession of motherhood for twenty-three years. Over the years she has augmented our income by teaching piano and voice in our home. More recently, she's helped by writing, speaking and leading Hearts at Home, which encourages, educates and equips moms.

It hasn't always been easy. Honestly, we've struggled to fulfill our commitment to provide our family with the things money can't buy when we've wished our family could have some of the things money *can* buy. Along the way we've battled consumerism, weighed the difference between needs and wants, and learned to live differently than many families around us live.

We've chosen to live with less, but in today's economy, many families have to live with less by default when a company closes, a job is eliminated, or an entire industry downsizes. You may have found yourselves at a place in life you never expected. At this cross-roads in life, you have to adjust your thinking to accommodate your circumstances. Our hope is to help you do that. To think differently about the word "downsizing." To consider the benefits found in living with less.

Whether a family is living with less by choice or by default, it is not necessarily a bad thing. With the right attitude, there is a different kind of joy, a different kind of pace, and a different kind of benefits package available to you and your family. Every time we've made the decision to live with less, we've found the little things we gain are really the things we've been yearning for all along.

DEFINING LESS

So just what is the "less" we are talking about? We have found three areas of our life that we can intentionally downsize:

- Less money—Are our financial challenges really about the high cost of living or the high cost of the way we choose to live? Where can we make different choices in our income and expenses that allow us to find the "more" we're actually looking for?

- Less stress—For many of us, life is lots of activity, an emphasis on overachievement and accomplishments, and moving up the ladder of success. But what if we defined success differently? What if we looked at accomplishment through a different lens? What if we made countercultural choices that actually resulted in less stress?
- Fewer activities—The world offers parents and children so many opportunities. But just because something is offered doesn't make it a wise choice for our children, our family, or us. What if we learned to say no more often? What if we created some healthy boundaries that kept us home and focused on family more?

THE REALITIES OF LESS

Living with less requires us to give up some things. Personally, we've found the sacrifice to be worth the benefits, but you need to consider the realities of what living with less means.

less money

In general, a family that lives with less may have less money coming into the household. Maybe you're living with less money by default, not by decision. Maybe you weren't planning on living with less, but that's the hand you've been dealt right now. If living with less is by decision, it could be because only one parent is working full-time in a two-parent home or because one parent is working full-time and the other part-time. It might be because one or both parents made the decision not to work overtime hours if given the option. It could be because one or both parents chose to work a less demanding job that keeps them more available to their family—but that also limits their ability to move up to posi tions that pay more. This might be the situation in a single home too.

Whatever the reason, having less money coming into the home brings about certain challenges and necessary sacrifices. We'll explore those sacrifices a little bit later, but suffice it to say that when there is less income coming in, there must be fewer expenses going out. Sometimes that means living in a smaller house, relocating to a different neighborhood, driving older cars, shopping in different stores, or choosing less expensive recreational activities. None of those will reduce our quality of life if we redefine "quality" based on relational benefits, not material things.

less insurance

Choosing to live on one income or move from full-time to part-time work could affect your family's insurance benefits. Health insurance is the biggest concern for most families considering making a lifestyle change, since group health insurance often costs less than an individual insurance policy. A family may have to figure that reality into their vision if they choose to live with less.

less to invest for the future

If there's less income to live on, there's obviously less income to invest for the future. A family would be unwise to disregard planning for the future, but they may need to adjust their expectations of what they can realistically contribute while raising a family. The earlier we start saving and investing, the better off we'll be in the long run as we let compound interest and/or the stock market do the work for us. We'll talk more about a diversified investment plan later in the book, but for now we'll simply acknowledge the realities of changed expectations and adjusted strategies that we need when we live with less income. In general, a family that lives with less has to see relational investments as just as important as or even more important than financial investments.

fewer promotions

Depending on how a family chooses to live with less, one loss could be the forgone ability to climb the corporate ladder. More demanding, higher-profile jobs come with great titles and generous salaries, but they may also require more hours, more travel and more stress. If you choose to limit your job possibilities in an effort to provide your family with more of you, the result may be fewer promotions and therefore less income over your lifetime.

fewer opportunities and activities

Living with less means choosing how to spend your time more wisely, and it may mean you'll lose out on some personal opportunities. I (Jill) have found this to be true when it comes to my love for musical theater. I'd love to audition for our local community-theater productions, but I choose not to in order to keep our family life more stable. I hate missing out on the fun, but it's a decision that will give my family more in the long run. You might say, "Well, Jill, you are giving yourself up for your family. That's not healthy. You don't want to lose yourself while raising a family." That's absolutely true, but I'm not losing myself. I'm just investing in hobbies and activities that take less prime time away from my family during this season. Musical theater will be there when my kids are grown.

LOSS IS GAIN

Our Roth IRA is barely growing, but our investment in the next generation is paying great dividends relationally. In fact, relational benefits are the "more" that we've discovered along the way. Understanding "less" is only part of the vision—the best part is in all we have to gain. There's more to life than what many of us are living.

Turn the page and let's take a look at how you can turn "loss" into incredible gain for your family.

Lord, we picked up this book for a reason. One (or both) of us is unsettled. We want something different, but we're not even sure what different really looks like. Help us to find a unified vision for our family. Show us new perspectives and new ways of thinking. Help us to open our hearts and minds to the attitudes and actions of living with less in order to gain a whole lot more. In Jesus' name, amen.

let's talk about it

The one thing that really made me think in this chapter is ...

When our kids are grown and gone, I hope to have provided for them ... (Share as many things as come to mind.)

My expectation about reading this book is ...

My fears about reading this book are ...

chapter 2

redefining more

IN CONSIDERING THE LESS-IS-MORE VISION, IT'S IMPORTANT TO LOOK AT WHAT WE MIGHT HAVE TO GIVE UP. But it's even more important for us to consider what we could gain in the process—the "more" that many of us are looking for.

THE BEAUTY OF "MORE"

When our daughter Anne lost her job due to the economy, she thought only in terms of what she and her husband would be losing, rather than what they might be gaining. She didn't discover what she had actually gained until after the transition. Her new life came with a different kind of benefits package, which she didn't even know was available to her.

Making changes to your family's work-life balance will alter more than just your paycheck. We've already looked at how choosing to live with less money for a season means we need to consider the ramifications of losing not only the income but also the benefits. But what new benefits package would we *gain* by not working overtime, getting off the slippery corporate ladder, limiting the number of activities our children participate in, or committing to having one parent available at home?

Remember, there *are* some things in this world that money can't buy. In making some of these changes, the new form of compensation will move from financial to relational. Let's look at the "more" you just might discover anytime you choose for your family to live with less.

more availability

Homemakers often get a bad rap, but the lost art of homemaking is making a comeback. Some of us are realizing that we can have it all, but just not all at once. In Jill's first book, *Professionalizing Motherhood*, she set about reframing mothering as the profession that it is. Helping moms to consider motherhood as a viable career choice and to think of it as a profession was the core message of this resource for moms. But honestly, that message needs to be one that both moms and dads understand. Because when you choose to live on less money, you have to have the shared vision for why you are making that choice. And you have to firmly believe that both partners carry equal responsibility, even if one person is bringing in the bulk of the income.

Healthy families are made up of people who have the time and energy to invest in the home and in family relationships. Raising children and nurturing a marriage take an incredible amount of time and energy—far more than most of us anticipate.

Parenting isn't the only consideration. Our friend Becky and her husband Dave have a grown son, but they still value Becky's being primarily at home: She is committed to the ministry of *availability*. Not only does she take care of their home and carry most of the responsibilities for meal preparation, but she also helps her aging parents, accompanies her husband to see specialists for his diabetes, provides a listening ear to friends from church, is available on occasion to assist their son, volunteers with Hearts at Home and mentors young moms. She is also available to speak to church groups that pay her for her time, a source of supplementary income that allows her to be flexible but still provides financially for the family. Becky contributes to the family's financial needs in other ways as well; for instance, she does it through savings—her availability allows her to shop wisely and watch her spending carefully.

Becky may not be contributing to a 401(k), but her investments pay out in relational dividends that really add value to her family and her community. That's something both she *and her husband* understand.

Availability is a flexible benefit that can provide for the family in rich and meaningful ways. Maybe the concept of the benefit of availability seems quite impractical. Hang in there and explore a little more with us. We promise to expand your vision for your family and introduce you to the attitudes and actions needed to make decisions—little and big—in favor of home and family.

more peace

When there are fewer demands on our time, there is more likely to be peace. But let's be honest—a life filled with kids can't often be described as peaceful. You might be able to experience it on the rare occasion when they're all sleeping at the same time, but even that is an infrequent occurrence. What we have found, however, is that when both of us have too much on our plates, it's hard to find peace even when the kids are sleeping!

We have to make sure our basic activity schedule leaves enough margin in our day for the unexpected to happen. Children often bring chaos, but adding too many activities, commitments and jobs to the mix can take that chaos to a higher level when real-life happens—like when Junior is sick or Shannon needs to go to the orthodontist for a midday appointment. Too many "good" volunteer responsibilities can even crowd out family time.

The truth is, the more we juggle, the less peace we have. Choosing to simplify by letting go of some of the demands brings us that much closer to reaping the benefits of peace. During the writing of this book, our family made some decisions that have already resulted in more peace, especially for Mark. The challenges of running two major ministries proved to be too stressful for our marriage and our family. In evaluating that, Mark initially made the decision to transition from his job as senior pastor of the church we started ten years ago to teaching pastor. The new title removed some of the responsibilities of "leading the leaders," which drained Mark of his time, passion and energy. The church determined that this transition would affect his pay. But just weeks into the new role, he found a sense of peace that he hasn't felt for a long time.

This decision was not easy to make. Mark has dealt with all the usual questions one considers: Am I giving up? Am I quitting too easily? Is this God's plan for my life? Is this failure? What really defines me? Where do I find my value? After asking all of those questions, he also had to ask: If I have fewer responsibilities at work, can I truly give more to my family? My marriage? Thus far, he feels that what he has gained outweighs what he gave up.

Peace happens when our external choices match our internal values. If we are living one way but our heart longs to live a different way, the resulting turmoil will rob us of the peace we desire.

more patience

Patience is a virtue that gets lost in the shuffle. Case in point: One evening, Jill stood in the kitchen preparing dinner while our twelve-year-old daughter peppered her with one question after another. After the fifth question in as many minutes, Jill was exasperated. "Erica," she said, "do you realize that you talk *nonstop*? Could you just be quiet for one minute?"

Immediately she was sick about that response. *Did I really just say that? And did it sound as impatient as I think it did?*

The answer was yes. Let's face it—we all blow it occasionally. Every one of us gives our children reasons to consult Dr. Phil. What we've found, however, is that patience takes energy, and energy is hard to come by when you feel stretched in too many directions.

Our friend Dustin works third shift and finds that fatigue often compromises his patience. While third shift can pay more in some jobs, Dustin says he really doesn't care. Moving to a day shift would mean less money, but it would also mean more sleep and more patience. Those are the "mores" he really wants for himself and for his family. As soon as a day shift comes available, he'll gladly make the change.

If you live with other people, it's not a matter of *if* patience is needed but a matter of *when*. Patience is one part self-control, one part endurance, and one part tolerance. If our physical and emotional reserves are spent, there's little left for patience when it is desperately needed. Living with fewer commitments and less stress—even if it sometimes means less money—can increase our capacity for patience. Patience is an essential benefit every parent needs in the midst of raising a family.

more kindness

Kindness is an important benefit that sometimes gets forgotten when life gets too busy. I realized this when one evening I picked up the phone and heard my husband's frustration: "Jill, I forgot my coffee!" It was 9:30 PM. He was on a summer camping trip with our two youngest sons, and he had just finished setting up the camper.

"Do you want me to bring you some?" I asked, honestly hoping he would say no. With the campground only twenty miles from our home, I certainly could, but I really didn't want to—I was sitting comfortably at home in my jammies. He responded that it wasn't necessary for me to make the trip, but that he just needed to vent. As soon as I hung up, I regretted my attitude.

I wavered back and forth between selfishness and kindness for a few minutes, but kindness eventually won out. My husband loves his coffee. While I don't share his addiction, er, affection, for the stuff, I know how much he appreciates a hot cup of coffee first thing in the morning. So I knew what I needed to do. I put on my street clothes, climbed in the car and drove to the campground to deliver his gift.

While a slower pace or a less complicated life won't assure kindness, it certainly helps to keep the emotional reserves at a healthy level to allow for kindness to happen. I know that there have been plenty of times when we've had too much on our plates, and choosing kindness took more emotional energy than it should have. I can remember times when I chose not to do the kind thing because I decided I was too tired of everyone sucking the life out of me and I just didn't have it in me to be nice. I've even heard one friend say, "I'm all out of nice." But relationships are damaged when we're "all out of nice." This happens when we fill our life with too many responsibilities and activities and we mistakenly feel that selfishness is the only right choice. When we make a choice to live with less stress, kindness is one of the many benefits we just might gain.

more joy

We've heard it said that happiness is an inside job, and we've found that this is true. Happiness comes from within us, not from the outside in. Our faith serves as a foundation for our life, and even if our circumstances change, our God doesn't. That's where true joy comes from.

But there's also a kind of joy that happens when life has a balance to it. This type of joy is found in seeing a baby's first steps or capturing the excitement of your first-grader in the first fifteen minutes after school. It's experienced while sitting on the porch swing with your spouse and dreaming together. It's found sitting around the dinner table laughing with your family and sharing about your day. It's even found in maintaining a strong sense of humor.

Let's face it, there are a lot of things our kids do that make us laugh. But when our emotional reserves are depleted, we lack this healthy perspective. We view the same children saying and doing the same silly things as frustrations.

"I stopped laughing," claimed one mom who chose to trade in her high heels and power suits for tennis shoes and blue jeans. "That's when I knew I was in trouble," she continued, "there was no joy in my heart and even laughing at my seven-year-old's silly knock-knock jokes was beyond me. I didn't have time for such foolishness."

By giving ourselves the emotional space to see life through a lens of humor, we find this benefit gives life to every family member, increases the grace and decreases the anger often found in everyday family life.

better health

Most of us try to steer clear of anything that has the ability to make us sick. To avoid germs, we wash our hands. To prevent food poisoning, we cook our meat properly. To keep our blood pressure and weight under control, many of us exercise. These are well-known guidelines for healthy living.

We rarely consider stress to be unhealthy, yet numerous studies have shown the negative effects of stress on health. A full 43 percent of US adults suffer adverse health effects from stress, according to an American Psychological Association (APA) study. Our friend Crystal, who is a physician assistant, confirms this: "Stress is a major contributor in health problems like tachycardia [fast heart rate] and irregular heart rhythms, high blood pressure, heart disease, anxiety, headaches, fibromyalgia, TMJ, ulcers, irritable bowel syndrome, chronic neck and back pain, higher susceptibility to viruses, and irregular menstrual periods."

You've likely heard the story of the frog that's put in a pot of cool water. The temperature is increased ever so slowly, and he doesn't realize he's boiling to death. He tolerates the slow increase in temperature and doesn't know he should get out until it's too late.

Many of us are like that frog. We didn't start out in the proverbial hot water, but the temperature has increased over time. We're swimming through the warm water, not even recognizing the death we are already experiencing in our relationships. And it's not just our relationships that suffer. Our physical health is often compromised, which can cost us not only energy but also time and money. But the drain is so slow and incremental that we hardly notice that it's happening.

A recent *Money* magazine article called "The Hidden Costs of Stress" stated, "Chronic stress, the kind you experience when the demands of life exceed your ability to cope, boosts the risk of developing ailments ranging from the common cold and gum disease to obesity and heart disease." The article puts the costs per year of stress at:

- $300 for over-the-counter drugs (e.g., pain relievers and decongestants)
- $5,600 for physician visits and other out-of-pocket health-care costs
- $375 for high life insurance premiums
- $500 or more for dental costs[1]

"But isn't stress just a way of life?" you might ask. If you talk to someone who has made choices to simplify, they'll tell you that stress doesn't have to be a way of life. Just ask our daughter Anne. If you had asked her if her two-hour commute added stress to her life,

[1] Gray, Patricia B., "The Hidden Costs of Stress," *Money*, December 2007: 44CKTK

she would have answered, "It's not a big deal." She even mentioned on a couple of occasions how she liked the drive there and back to "clear her head." But after the commute was removed from her life, she felt an immediate physical change. It was as if she could breathe deeper once it was no longer a part of her daily routine.

When work or home life is simplified or a family chooses to bring Mom or Dad home part-time or full-time, our health can be positively affected in several ways. We tend to eat better because someone is more available to cook meals rather than grabbing dinner at the drive-thru. We may have more time to exercise because both of us aren't burning the candle at both ends. We tend to sleep better because we're not up half the night trying to get the laundry done or the bills paid. The result of this benefit is that our immune system gets the boost it so desperately needs.

more organization

Both Todd and Sandy were working full-time and carrying major responsibilities at church. They were doing a great job with their volunteer positions, but their home life and their family were suffering from the stress of spinning too many plates. Laundry wasn't getting done, bills were paid late and their home had been relegated to being a drop-off location for mail and a site to sleep rather than a place of rest and relaxation for them to enjoy each other. After they both resigned from their high-responsibility volunteer positions, they found their "life" again. Each discovered a place to serve at church that required fewer meetings and preparation work. Home organization was regained and relational energy was restored.

As a recovering "messy," Jill has come to understand that organization takes more time than she realized. When both of us were working full-time outside the home, we had an extremely hard time keeping up with laundry, bills, housekeeping, cooking and dishes. And that was even before we had kids! We know there are families where both parents work outside the home, and they do just fine keeping up with these tasks, but we found the balancing act too difficult.

I know the relief it brings to me knowing that Jill is picking up the kids after school, overseeing homework and getting a start on dinner. And when Jill has something going on, I am able to re-arrange my schedule to cover the home front. Times like these give me a peek into just how much work it is to keep the family organized and running smoothly. Jill's contributions to our family's income are found when we outsource less and do-it-yourself more. Home orga-nization is one benefit we've experienced as a result of our decision.

more energy and intentionality for parenting

Kids need more than a present parent; they need an intentional parent. And intentionality takes an enormous amount of energy. An intentional parent has a vision for how they want to see their grown-up children living their lives. The intentional parent makes deliberate decisions because of their farsightedness, their vision.

Both of us grew up in very different family environments. When we started our family, our expectations of what parenting should or should not look like created more conflict between us than we liked. It wasn't until we took a parenting course through our church that we finally found ourselves sharing a vision for our family. No longer battling one another, we valued the same strategies and were working toward the same goals. The unity was refreshing and empowering.

When we're stretched too thin, our parenting is negatively af-fected and we can sometimes unintentionally step into some inef-fective parenting styles. Child-centered parenting often comes out of the guilt we experience when we have limited time with the child. We hate to take any time away from them either to take care of ourselves or to take care of our marriage. However, when our whole world revolves around our child, it's not healthy for us or for them.

Permissive parenting happens when we lack the energy to be consistent. It also happens when we feel we have so little time with our kids that we hate to use that time to correct them. We overlook misbehaviors in an effort to keep the peace and not ruin the moment.

Authoritarian parenting happens when we lack the time or the emotional capacity to be patient, loving and consistent in our direction and discipline. Authoritarian parents motivate with anger and produce obedience by fear. Because love feels conditional, children of authoritarian parents often equate success in school or sports with love.

Children do need authority in their lives. Understanding boundaries and having those boundaries enforced contributes to their sense of security. Children thrive under authoritative—not authoritarian—parenting. This is when a parent develops a close and nurturing relationship with their children while keeping a balance of expectations, rules and guidelines. Authoritative parenting takes energy and intentionality and it is a "more" that every child needs.

more energy and intentionality in marriage

Parenting isn't the only place that a family needs intentionality and energy. Marriage needs it as well. We remember sitting at a marriage conference when the speaker asked, "Where do you want your marriage to be in twenty years? How do you want to feel about each other after the kids are grown and gone? What investments do you need to make now so your love can last a lifetime?" These are questions that deserve some well-thought-out answers.

Our marriage has certainly had its highs and lows. At our lowest of lows we both declared that we did not love each other. We felt nothing but disdain for one another. That was the darkest season of both of our lives. It's a place to which we hope never to return.

During that difficult time we chose to pursue professional counseling, and it was the wisest thing we did. As we sorted through our issues as well as the baggage we both carried into our marriage, it became obvious that we had made an almost fatal mistake: We had put our children before our marriage. We didn't see it in the routine of life, but each day our lack of marriage intentionality contributed to a pattern of focusing on our kids and neglecting our relationship. We were enabling the slow erosion of our intimacy. In the same way that the waves eat away at the beach one grain of sand at a time until it's nearly nonexistent, we had moved from talking about hopes and dreams to diapers and dishes—our intimacy was disappearing, nibbled down by our routine. We lacked the vision that we desperately needed for our marriage to make it in the long haul. We also lacked the ability to see how our daily choices were hurting our marriage.

Our determination to simplify our life eventually proved that less equals more when it comes to our marriage. Less stress gives us more patience. Fewer commitments give us more time. Less criticism opens the door for more grace and forgiveness.

more attentiveness

"Mommy, listen to me with your eyes," our four-year-old son said one afternoon while he was telling Jill a story. She assured him she had heard every word he said, but she also realized that her lack of eye contact didn't communicate to him that he was valuable. She was trying to do too much at once. She needed to do less and to focus on him more, listening with her ears and watching with her eyes.

We can't cultivate relationships on autopilot. As much as we want to sometimes—wouldn't it be easier?—it just doesn't work.

We have to be attentive not just to our own needs but also to those of the people around us. And in order to be attentive, we have to have enough mental and emotional energy to tune in.

Have you ever been "listening" to a family member when you suddenly realize that you haven't heard a word they said? Most often that happens when we have too much on our minds. By removing some of the things we have to think about, we are more likely to be in tune with the family members we love. This benefit speaks love and value to those who mean the most to us.

more time

"Mom, will you tell me a story?" This is a question our youngest son asks almost every night when we tuck him in bed. He loves stories about our childhood years. He loves to hear stories about when we were dating. He enjoys stories that happened before he was born. But there's no way to shortcut a good story. It takes time— more time, unfortunately, than I usually want to offer at 9:00 PM. But time is what our son, like most children, longs for. Time is a gift we can give him. And quite frankly, one day he'll head to bed and he won't ask for a story anymore. We'll happily give the time as long as he desires it.

Relationships take time. Kids need Mom and Dad's time—lots of it. *Good Housekeeping* featured a quote from actor Will Smith regarding some insight he discovered about spending time with your kids: "While making the film *The Pursuit of Happyness*, my son Jaden, who was my costar, and I got to spend every single day, ten to twelve hours a day, together. It became clear that whatever you have to offer financially doesn't matter. Whatever situation you're in, it doesn't matter. You have to be there. You have to be with your child...To be able to spend that many hours a day together, our bond took off in a way that I never imagined."[2]

---

[2] "Good Buzz: Turning Point," *Good Housekeeping*, June 2008: 58.

Most of us don't have the luxury of working with our child like Will Smith does in Hollywood. But there are many strategies that normal families like yours and ours can do to intentionally spend time with our children. We can turn off the television and play a game with them. We can choose a walk to the park with our family rather than turning on the computer. We can turn off our cell phone and refrain from checking e-mail or text messages when we're home with our family. Rather than buying season tickets to our favorite sports team's games, we can set up a regular schedule to take our spouse on a date.

Families need time. Parenting takes time. A marriage needs regular investments of time to pay the love dividends that last a lifetime. You simply can't take a shortcut with this benefit—the quality versus quantity argument doesn't hold water here. Relationships need adequate time for us to build the deep intimacy we all long for. Choosing less over more can help us find the time to nurture our relationship with God and our family.

more margin

"The reality is that I have two full-time jobs," one weary mom shared while attending a Hearts at Home conference. "I have my job that brings home a paycheck, and I have my job taking care of my home and my family." She continued to reveal how she felt as if her husband and children got her leftovers rather than her best. She was tired, impatient and overwhelmed.

She's not alone. Many parents find themselves coming up short when it comes to having their best energy and efforts devoted to raising their family. If we do manage to balance work and home, there are often other areas of life that suffer—friendships, links to one's church family, ties with our neighbors.

Dr. Richard Swenson calls this lack of space in our lives "margin." In his book *Margin*, Dr. Swenson explains that, in the same way that a book has white space on the top and sides that allow us to enjoy the words on the page, our lives need enough "white space" so that we can enjoy relationships to their fullest. Too many of us run from one activity to another. Our kids are involved in so many extracurricular activities that they often don't know how to just play a pickup game of softball in the backyard. Similarly, many parents don't know how to interact with their family unless they have some organized activity to foster the relationship or ease the conversation.

Our fast-paced lives have to be managed by extensive "to do" lists that reprogram us into thinking that any activity not on a "to do" list is simply a waste of time. This might include playing dolls with our preschooler, going for a walk with our spouse, or grabbing a Coke with our teenager and just talking. Parents need adequate margins in their lives to allow for spontaneous interaction with their spouse and children. Children need enough unstructured time to foster their imagination and conquer boredom on occasion. Families need enough white space to play together, laugh together and enjoy—and grow—their relationships.

DECISIONS

So what do you think? Do the "mores" form a melody that you'd like to sing more often? Would you like to further explore the attitudes and actions that will take you there? In order to find this new benefits package, you do have to make some decisions. For many of us, these may be some of the hardest decisions we ever make. What makes them so difficult is that they are really about trading tangible benefits for intangible relationships.

Here are some real-life decisions men and women like us have made to live with less and give their best to their family:

- Bill chose to give up overtime hours and the resulting pay in exchange for being more available to his family.

- Mike opted off the corporate fast track in order to give his family stability by keeping them in one location and to ensure his workplace stress levels stayed manageable.
- Lori and her husband Bob chose to move to a significantly smaller home to give the family more financial margin, allow her to be home with the kids and relieve her husband from the weight of working extra hours to pay for their supersized life.
- Maria, who was working full-time and pursuing a college degree while raising two children, decided to delay finishing her education until she was in the empty-nest season of life, when it wouldn't cost so much relationally.
- Josh and Diana decided to live on Josh's income to allow Diana to devote her best time and energy to home and family responsibilities.
- Todd and Sue made the choice to live on Sue's income while Todd managed the home front and focused on their family.
- Mike and Lori agreed that Mike would give up his successful flooring business to work for an established company. This provided financial stability and greatly decreased stress.

Families who have chosen to live on less, opt out of life's rat race and increase their margin often find new energy, joy and peace they didn't even know they were missing. We've heard their stories personally through our speaking and our work with Hearts at Home and they consistently report more patience, which results in a more loving, gracious home environment.

So what do you think? How much white space is in your life? Your marriage? Your family? Your answers to these questions will help you evaluate if you need to consider making some "less" decisions in your life:

- Do you sit down at the table and eat dinner together as a family at least five times each week?   Yes   No
- Do you spend time actively playing with your children most days?   Yes   No
- Do you have a regular date time with your spouse weekly or monthly?   Yes   No
- Do you spend time with God on a daily basis?   Yes   No
- Do you exercise at least three times a week?   Yes   No
- Do you actively pursue and engage in friendships?   Yes   No
- Do you pursue hobbies or activities that you personally enjoy on occasion?   Yes   No
- Are you serving as a volunteer in your community and/or your church?   Yes   No

If you answered "No" to four or more of the above questions, you might want to check the speedometer of your life to see if you need to reduce your speed and enjoy the relationships that life is really all about.

CATCHING THE VISION?

We hope you're starting to catch the vision that less can actually be more. It's certainly a different perspective than you'll find in most of America, which is why we'll spend the next two sections of the book helping you explore the attitudes and the actions you'll need to live counterculturally and to battle adult peer pressure.

We didn't think about all this when we said "I do." The vision for what we wanted our family relationships to look like began to take shape in those eighteen months while we did day care in our home, but even then, we certainly didn't understand what we would need to do to make it a reality. We learned many lessons in the school of hard knocks. Over time, we've come to understand that the vision we have for our family—the benefits package we desperately want—requires an adjustment of attitude and an intentionality of actions.

An abundance of availability, peace, patience, kindness, joy, health, laughter, organization, attentiveness, energy, time and margin are just a few of the benefits you can find when you develop a vision to pursue life with a focus more on relationships than resources. This benefits package allows a family to enjoy the people who are most important to them. If you're raising a family, it gives you the time and energy needed to invest in your marriage and parenting with intentionality.

Are you ready to learn more about how to actually live with less? It's not always easy to make it happen, but it's also not impossible. Regardless of where you are in the process—not yet convinced or already learning to live with less—there is still value in exploring both the attitudes and the actions that both moms and dads need to keep their heads, hearts and bodies at home as much as possible.

Lord, we really do want more. More of You. More for our family. Help us see the right kind of loss as gain. We may not be sure how to live with less, but we want at least to explore the possibilities. Touch our hearts and renew our minds to catch the vision You have for our family! In Jesus' name, amen.

let's talk about it

Three benefits I would like to see implemented in our family are...

I long for more _____ in our marriage.

I would love for our family to _____ more often.

part 2: attitudes

MOST PARENTS WILL AT SOME POINT TELL THEIR
CHILD TO "GET RID OF THE ATTITUDE." They're
reacting to the eye rolling, the deep sighing and the "you just don't
understand" body language that usually emerge sometime around
junior high.

Oh yes—we know all about attitude.

But the kinds of attitudes we're going to be talking about in this
section have nothing to do with eye rolling and everything to do
with vision. If you are a single parent, we want you to firmly grasp
the attitudes you'll need to have to wholeheartedly pursue your vision for your family. If you are married, we want to help you and
your spouse develop a shared vision for your partnership.

This section of the book will explore the components—the
attitudes—that make up the "living with less" mindset. These aren't
attitudes we need to get rid of; these are attitudes that will help
us live out the vision we have for our family. Turn the page and
continue the adventure of redefining your family's priorities!

chapter 3

countercultural mindset: it's an out-of-this-world experience

LET'S BE HONEST AND GET AN UNCOMFORTABLE FACT RIGHT OUT THERE: Mark will be the first to admit that he has far more trouble with "today in light of eternity" than Jill does. Being content with what we have on this earth is sometimes a struggle. And wanting the newest gadget, tool, toy—we're talking big boy toys like motorcycles, yard equipment, etc.—seems to be Mark's downfall. Of course it's hard to live with less when everyone else appears to have more. Not only that, but living in this advertisement-saturated culture drives our desire for what we don't have. Those ads sometimes even go so far as to insinuate that we are foolish if we try to live without certain things. So if we struggle with this personally, our culture certainly doesn't do much to help us.

How do we battle all those wants? How can we move our hearts away from things and focus them more on people? How do we keep an eternity-minded perspective when the here and now is so real, so tangible and so seemingly desirable? Can we really keep jealousy and covetousness at bay? Is it possible to believe that less really is more? In this chapter we'll explore the inner recesses of our heart, our relationship with God, and understanding what drives our wants. Doing so will help us to live out a countercultural vision for our family.

WHERE IT ALL BEGINS

God wants us to be fully sold out—to Him. He longs for us to recognize that who we are and what we have fully belongs to Him. Why is this important? Because God can do way more with our lives and our talents and our stuff than we ever could alone! And His strength and vision far surpass our own. That's hard for us to comprehend, but it's the truth. And if you and I are going to fight the prevailing culture, we're going to need more strength than we have on our own.

Before we launch any further into our discussion, let's make sure we're understanding the fundamentals that underpin everything else that we'll tackle. The God of the universe created you and me and everyone else to be in relationship with Him. Because He would never force Himself on us, He has given us free will. That means that while He longs for relationship with us, He allows us to make our own choices about whether we want that relationship with Him. God loves us so much that He sent His son Jesus to earth to show us the way and ultimately give His life for us. He died so we can live.

Jesus has reached his hand out to us. The question is whether we have chosen to take it or not. If we try to live life without a relationship with our Creator, we'll always come up short; that kind of living with less will make the kind we're talking about even harder—and perhaps near impossible. That's because we need more courage, more strength and more hope than what we have on our own to turn our vision of "less" into reality. Trying to live life without God and His Truth is like purchasing a complicated appliance for the home and never reading the instruction book. We may use that appliance to the fullness of our knowledge and abilities, but we'll never use it to the fullness of *its* abilities. Why? Because we don't know what we don't know! A whole new world of wisdom and truth opens up to us when we say yes to God.

I (Mark) said yes to God at a Billy Graham crusade. When I was growing up, my family had little to do with church. As a twenty-two-year-old, I was living a dead-end life that seemed great fun on the outside, but was coming up empty on the inside. As I sat at a bar late one night I said to God, "There's got to be more to life than this." It was just a few days later that I found myself sitting in a stadium with thousands of other people. I went to see Billy Graham as a favor to my mom. But it was as if Billy Graham had pulled up a chair and was talking just to me. He answered every question I had. My life has never been the same since.

I (Jill) went to church my entire life. My parents established a foundation of faith for me early in life, but it wasn't until freshman year of college that I transitioned from "religion" to "relationship." When I said yes to God, I found the Bible offered the wisdom I desperately needed and God's Spirit provided the direction I longed for. This was the first time I was actually introduced to the less-is-more concept; I began to catch God's vision for "less of me and more of Him" (John 3:30).

God has so much more for us in this life if we choose to live it in relationship with Him. His knowledge, strength and abilities far supersede ours. So have you said yes to God? If you haven't, let's start there today. Have a conversation with God that goes something like this, *"God, it's me. I've tried to do this thing on my own, but I realize that my resources are limited and Yours are unlimited. I want to learn to live life Your way, even though, quite honestly, that's scary in some ways. I'm sorry that I've tried to live on my own and made so many mistakes along the way. I ask for Your forgiveness and the opportunity to start over again. Thank You for sending Your Son Jesus to show me the way to You. I accept Him as my Savior. And I want to learn how to let Him lead in my life. In Jesus' name, amen.*

If you just prayed that prayer for the first time, let us know. We'd love the opportunity to encourage you further. Today is the first day

of the rest of your life and a whole new world has just opened up
to you!

LET GOD DO THE DRIVING

Once we say yes to God, we can spend the rest of our lives building
our friendship with Him. Having a relationship with God is to enjoy
a friendship with someone who can not just see the future but also
shape it. This is especially valuable for those of us living the less-is-
more life, which often demands that we walk by faith. God knows
the twists and turns ahead of us. He knows the character building
that needs to take place in our lives to weather those twists and turns.
And because of that, He's better equipped to drive through life than
any of us are. But let's be honest: turning over the steering wheel of
our lives is harder than it looks. We like to be in control. We like
to call the shots. Unfortunately, we do a poor job compared to what
God can do.

God has so much for us to learn, but He's not advertising it on
billboards or on prime-time TV commercials. We're going to have
to dig a little deeper and make a little more effort to learn God's
ways and apply His truth to our life. This applies to us individually,
as couples and as families. So where do we begin? We have to begin
by taking one step at a time.

step 1: look to the word

The Bible is God's letter to us. It's His truth for our lives. But we
have to dig in and mine for the gold He has for us. A miner would
never just walk into a cave, take a look around and say, "Hmm. Don't
see any gold here." We can't just open God's Word, read a few lines
and say, "I don't see anything that applies to me." A miner takes
his pick and ax and begins chipping away to find the gold. We all
have to do that with God's Word. We have to stay committed and
keep digging.

A good place to start is the book of Proverbs. There are thirty-one chapters in Proverbs and thirty-one days in seven of the twelve months. If, every day, you read the chapter of Proverbs that corresponds to that day of the month, you'll find incredible wisdom for your life—and the repetition, month after month, will help you remember it. For instance, Proverbs 3:5–6 (*The Message*) has this wisdom: "Trust God from the bottom of your heart; don't try to figure out everything on your own. Listen for God's voice in everything you do, everywhere you go; he's the one who will keep you on track." Proverbs 11:2 (NLT) tells us, "Pride leads to disgrace, but with humility comes wisdom."

Once you've gotten into the habit of digging into Proverbs daily, add one New Testament chapter each day. The book of Luke is a good place to start. If you read one chapter of Proverbs and one other chapter of the Bible, it should take you ten to fifteen minutes a day. That's honestly not much time in the grand scheme of things.

The Bible has so much wisdom for the less-is-more life! Check out these nuggets of truth just from the sixth chapter of the book of Matthew:

> Don't hoard treasure down here where it gets eaten by moths and corroded by rust or—worse!—stolen by burglars. Stockpile treasure in heaven, where it's safe from moth and rust and burglars. It's obvious, isn't it? The place where your treasure is, is the place you will most want to be, and end up being. Matthew 6:19–21 (*The Message*)

> You can't worship two gods at once. Loving one god, you'll end up hating the other. Adoration of one feeds contempt for the other. You can't worship God and Money both. Matthew 6:24 (*The Message*)

> Give your entire attention to what God is doing right now, and don't get worked up about what may or may not happen

tomorrow. God will help you deal with whatever hard things come up when the time comes. Matthew 6:34 (*The Message*)

Those words may have been written some two thousand years ago, but they are no less relevant today. We need God's truth in our lives. When would reading God's Word fit into your day? First thing in the morning, maybe even before you get out of bed? During breakfast? On the train to work? During your child's nap time in the afternoon? In the evening before you go to bed? What if you and your spouse read the chapters aloud together? There's no right way or right time except what is right for you. The important thing isn't when—it's that you do it! The more God's truth sinks into your heart and mind, the easier it will be to let Him lead you through this less-is-more journey.

step 2: listen to the spirit

The more we talk to God, the more comfortable we become in the relationship. But God wants to have conversation with us, and conversation is never just one-sided. God speaks to us in several ways. Let's look at each one.

The first way God speaks to us is through what one might call a "nudge." It's that moment when a thought comes into your mind that definitely is not yours. It might be a very random thought prompting you to do something that seems rather foolish. For instance, one Sunday morning Jill had a "nudge" from God to go speak to someone in her Sunday-school class. But her sense wasn't to wait until after Sunday school—it was to do it right then, in the middle of the teacher's lesson. She fought with God in her mind: "That's crazy, God. I'm not going to disrupt class. I'm not going to take her focus off of the teacher." But God didn't let up. He impressed upon Jill the need to go—right then and there. She quietly got up out of her seat. Luckily this person was sitting on the aisle, so Jill could crouch down beside her and tell her that she sensed God wanted the two of them to connect. The tears began to fall, so Jill suggested stepping out into the hall. As soon as they were out of the classroom, the woman told Jill through her tears that her husband had left her that morning. She was barely holding it together and certainly wasn't getting anything out of that morning's lesson. They went and found a quiet place to sit, talk and pray. God knew what she needed and He asked Jill to trust Him. That's the power of a "holy nudge."

When it comes to our downsized life, we've known God to nudge us to stop at a garage sale only to find the exact thing we've been asking Him to help us find. And one time Jill was prompted to drive home from church a different way than she usually drives. Our family had been without a dishwasher for nine months because we couldn't afford to replace it. We'd been praying, though. And here was a man rolling a perfectly good dishwasher out to the road with a "$50" sign on it. God's nudge resulted in our provision!

God also speaks through other people. One day while we were in the process of adopting our son Kolya, Jill found herself sitting across the table in a Panera Bread restaurant from her friend Julie. Jill told Julie that we knew Kolya was ours, but we honestly didn't have one dime to make it happen—the words "financial suicide" might have been used to describe what we feared we would be facing. Julie sat and listened, and then she shared some powerful words: "Jill, our God owns the cattle on a thousand hills. He just needs to sell a few cows to make this happen!"

That truth, based upon Psalm 50:10, was exactly what Jill needed to hear then and there. God spoke to us through Julie that day. And then He began selling cows—dozens of them, in fact. We did a family fundraiser that raised $5,000 and then learned about a matching-grant program that doubled that. Within the first two months of our making the decision to adopt, God sold $10,000 worth of cows!

Another $9,000 came in within the next two months from friends and family, another grant, and another fundraiser our daughter created called "Cooking for Kolya." But we were still short $15,000 for the $36,000 adoption fee.

It was in providing for this final need that God really blew us away. One day, we received a $15,000 check in the mail...from a complete stranger! That day God sold a whole herd of cows.

A third way that God speaks to us is through His Word—the Holy Bible. I (Mark) have struggled with self-confidence throughout my life. Questions such as "Who am I?" and "Why am I so powerless?" tormented me. One day, I was poring over the Bible and read this passage in Ephesians: "I pray that your hearts will be flooded with light so that you can understand the confident hope he has given to those he called—his holy people who are his rich and glorious inheritance. I also pray that you will understand the incredible greatness of God's power for us who believe him. This is the same mighty power that raised Christ from the dead and seated him in the place of honor at God's right hand in the heavenly realms." (Ephesians 1:18–20, NLT) When I read and received these words, my life began to change. I was powerless because I had chosen not to live in that incredibly great power God had given me.

If we allow it, God's Word can speak to us very clearly. And we need that truth and wisdom even more if we're trying to live a life that is different than that of much of the world.

step 3: lean into community

We need to be around people who will encourage us in our relationships with God. Most of us will likely find such encouragement in a church family—and even more intimately in a small group. Sometimes we'll find it in one-on-one relationships that encourage us in God's truth (as Jill's friend Julie did) and that hold us accountable as well. We need that accountability because we don't always see things accurately. We need the shared perspective and wisdom of others to bring balance to thoughts and actions.

We also need prayer partners. We need people who will pray for us when we are in such a tough position that we don't know how to pray for ourselves. We need friends who will pray for our kids when they are making wrong choices. We need friends who will pray for us when we are making wrong choices—and kick us in the seat of the pants, so to speak, when we need it, which is the beauty of accountability! We need friends who will pray for us even when things seem to be going well, that we would know the source of our blessing and our strength. And we need friends who will pray that we stay true to our "less is more" lifestyle even when—and especially when—our resolve is being worn down by the world.

If you're married, community starts in your marriage. Share with each other, trust one another, and pray with and for each other. This will strengthen your partnership and embolden you jointly as you seek to live out your vision for your family.

We're not designed to experience this life journey alone. Even Jesus lived life with a small group of fellow travelers, whom we most often call the disciples. They spent time learning about God, praying and reaching out to the world together. If that's the way Jesus lived, then that's the example He set for us!

step 4: expect heart surgery

Once we've said yes to Jesus and we're on our lifelong journey to grow our friendship with Him, we have to begin to allow Him to bring conviction to our hearts and minds when we need it. Notice we said "conviction," not "condemnation." God convicts our hearts— which means He shows us what and where we need to change. Sometimes conviction shows us when we were wrong, prompting us to apologize and ask forgiveness of God or others.

It is so easy to look at someone else's supersized life and get a case of the "wants"—especially if we're striving to live the "less is more" lifestyle. We need to allow God to do heart surgery. To try to keep up with the Joneses—even mentally, by comparing our house to another family's or our car to the neighbor's—is to enter the land of covetousness. When we want what someone else has, it can twist our hearts and throw us into the sins of envy, jealousy and coveting.

These three words are very close in meaning, but each has a slightly different angle to it. Envy is when we feel resentful and unhappy because we want something that someone else has, whether something they own or something they have achieved. Jealousy is a feeling of resentment that someone else has gained something you feel you rightfully deserve. And to covet is simply to want something someone else has. Coveting must be a pretty big deal to God because He included it in the Ten Commandments. Exodus 20:17 (NIV) says, "You shall not covet your neighbor's house. You shall not covet your neighbor's wife...or anything that belongs to your neighbor."

When we recognize sin in our hearts, it's time to allow God to do heart surgery. This starts with conviction (I'm wrong). Then it moves into confession (I did this). Next, it progresses into repentance (I'm sorry). And finally it ends with receiving forgiveness (I'm forgiven). God desires to forgive us when we're wrong, but again, we have to ask. Saying "I'm sorry, and will you please forgive me?"—to God or anyone else we have wronged—helps us to begin to make more permanent changes in our lives. The more we have to clean up our messes, the less likely we are to make the same mess over and over.

STICK WITH GOD

When our kids entered their teen years, we made it very clear that anytime they face peer pressure, we are willing to be the bad guys. If they are at a party where people are drinking, an announcement that "my parents just called and I have to go home" will work just fine. They can use us as an out to extract themselves from a bad situation. We do that because we understand that sometimes we all need a little more strength than we have on our own.

Living a lifestyle that is different from the world's comes with its own peer pressure. And, just like our teens, we can't win this battle alone. We need God's strength to bolster our resolve and boost our courage to do things differently than the majority. We need His clear perspective on what's really important when our point of view gets clouded. We need His truth when the world's lies taint our perception. We need His voice to cut through the noise of this world and give us the direction we need for our family. We can really have an out-of-this-world experience living counterculturally if we stick with God.

Father God, I do want to learn how to let You into the driver's seat of my life. Help me to live by conviction, not by my circumstances. Give me strength when I'm facing pressure from this world. And help me to stay steady in You because while my circumstances may change, You never will. I want to look to Your Word, listen to Your Spirit and lean into the community that You have placed around me. That's the firm foundation I want to build my life on. In Jesus' name, amen.

let's talk about it

After reading this chapter, I've really been thinking about . . .

When it comes to letting God lead my life, my biggest fear is . . .
In order to let God do the driving, the step I most need to consider is . . .

chapter 4

contentment: living with less and liking it

WE'D SPENT THE ENTIRE WEEK IN EL SALVADOR.
Mark had stayed home to take care of our sons, but each day Anne,
Erica and I, along with the rest of our group, visited poverty-fighting
Compassion International projects in nearly one hundred-degree
heat. We laughed with little ones who were missing their front teeth.
We talked with moms with our broken Spanish. We blew bubbles,
braided hair and painted faces.

Each day we also had the sobering opportunity to participate in
a home visit. Most days these visits broke my heart. The realities
of living in poverty stared me right in the face inside these homes.
These weren't pictures of starving kids. These starving kids were
standing right in front of me.

"What is the opposite of poverty?" asked the Compassion staff
member at the closing event of the week. "Wealth," I answered
silently in my mind. Wealth seemed to be the logical answer to that
question.

But it wasn't the correct answer. "The opposite of poverty," he
said, "is enough." I think you could have heard a pin drop in the
room. It seemed to be a new idea for every one of us.

I thought back over our week of seeing poverty firsthand and up
close. He was right—you didn't need to be wealthy to live outside
of poverty. You simply needed to have enough. Enough to eat that
you weren't malnourished. Enough health-care that you didn't have

parasites in your stomach. Enough money to provide a roof over your family's head and food for the table.

Most of us live in places that have more than enough, and quite honestly that makes us wealthy. I've never considered myself wealthy in forty-four years of life. I grew up in a family that was comfortable; while we would have never been considered wealthy by American standards, we were in the global sense. Mark and I scrimp, pinch pennies and have done without during much of our twenty-six-plus years of marriage and raising a family. There have been many times when we've wondered whether we'll make it financially. It has seemed hard. But we've always had enough—and in fact we've had more than enough. We just haven't realized it because we're so rarely confronted with someone who really doesn't have enough.

Suffice it to say, that trip completely changed our family's view of what contentment—and enough—really means.

MORE THAN ENOUGH

If we truly have more than enough, why doesn't it feel that way to most of us? Why do we feel we need more food, more house, more car, more money and more clothes? As we've had to grapple with such questions, we've come to understand there are three reasons why most of us struggle to be content. Let's explore these to see if they apply to us in any way.

1. we believe the siren call of advertising

In Greek mythology, the Sirens were three beautiful, seductive women who sang their beautiful songs to lure sailors to their island. The men were invariably entranced. They couldn't resist drawing nearer to the sweet song, and ended up shipwrecked on the rocky shores. In today's culture, advertising has a similar draw for us.

We're enticed by the right words, the right colors and even the right music.

We're writing this chapter during a one-week Florida vacation. Even today I (Jill) found myself drawn into the advertising hype as we drove to our favorite, free snorkeling site in Destin, Florida. "Sail Aboard Blackbeard's Pirate Ship," called one sign. *My boys would so love that experience!* I thought to myself—even though a cruise like that isn't in our family vacation budget.

A few blocks down the road, we happened upon Krispy Kreme, and the "Hot Donuts" sign was brightly lit. *Mmmmm. Krispy Kremes sounds so good!* In fact our daughter Erica saw the sign and immediately said, "Can we stop at Krispy Kreme?"

And then right next to Krispy Kreme was a beach store having a huge sale. "Everything $5 or less!" screamed the big banners. *Wow, what a great sale!* I thought to myself. *Maybe we ought to stop.* Then I realized there wasn't a single thing I could think of that we would need at a beach shop. The advertising was doing its job well, drawing my mind and my senses into its siren call.

Is there nowhere to turn without being assaulted by advertising? Think about it. If you go to a movie, you'll watch a half-hour of straight product advertising followed by movie trailers advertising even more movies before the film you actually want to see begins. When you're on your computer, pop-up ads pester you anytime you surf the Internet. When watching an hourlong show on television you'll see about twenty minutes of commercials. In grocery stores, there are ads on the child seats on the grocery carts, coupon machines right in the aisles, and "sale" signs blasting you with the "best" deals. And have you ever noticed the little plastic baton that separates your groceries from the next customer's groceries on the conveyor belt? Yep! You'll find advertising there too! Even the savviest shoppers can get worn down into buying all kinds of things we really don't need or don't have the money for.

2. *we get introduced to "something better"*

Just the other night the Savage family was introduced to HD television. High-definition television has been around for quite some time, but honestly none of us had ever seen it. While staying at Jill's parents' condo in Florida, we were experimenting with their new HDTV. With the remote you could move between a regular picture and a high-definition picture. Our daughter Erica pointed it out and showed us the difference. We were amazed at the clarity in the HD picture! Suddenly our regular picture back home looked awfully fuzzy. But we'd never thought it was fuzzy until we saw something better—and this new experience caused us to be discontent with what we have.

There's another side to "new and better" to be considered. While in Florida, we decided to watch one of our favorite movies on DVD. While we've seen it a half dozen times, we chose, of course, to watch the movie in high definition this time. During the opening scenes several of us exclaimed, "Wow, look how fake that background is! I've never noticed that before."

Of course we hadn't. We'd only watched the movie on our plain old non-HD television. We all agreed that maybe HD wasn't all that great; better isn't always really the best.

Some of you guys might be indignant after reading that about HD. Mark loves technology and the latest and greatest. And we're not saying you shouldn't have HD. We are saying that we have had to learn to look at our wants and weigh those against not only our wallets but also our bigger vision for our family. For us, a new television is not in the budget right now. Our newly married son just purchased a new flat-screen HDTV. At the end of that purchase he was informed that his DVD player wouldn't work with the HDTV. He then had to purchase a new DVD player too. The costs pile up. The things we want because we're discontent often come with unexpected costs, and we have to consider those as well.

3. we get caught up in the comparison trap

A small child always seems to want the toy another child has in his hand. The comparison trap starts early, doesn't it? And we don't really seem to grow out of it. Our human nature naturally hunts out and sniffs out what toys others have that we don't. We have our own perfectly good toys, but someone else has something new or slightly different and suddenly we want it too!

We're all tempted to compare our lives to the lives of others. There are, however, some strategies that we can deploy proactively to help ourselves stop longing for what we don't have. Try putting into practice these five ways to conquer comparisons.

First, develop a thankful attitude. Many times we're unhappy not because we aren't doing well, but because we think others are doing better. Instead of looking at what others have, let's move our eyes to what we have. And let's start thanking God for those things every day.

Second, establish a reasonable standard of living. We need to develop our lifestyle based upon our convictions, not our circumstances. Wherever God has you financially, stay committed to living within your means. Learning to live within a predetermined budget is important.

Third, learn to discern between wants and needs. Needs are the basics—food, clothing, shelter and health care. Wants are anything beyond the basics. The world screams to us that wants are actually needs: Every child needs this toy, every dad needs this tool, and every mom deserves this kitchen appliance. But the definitions of needs and wants must come from you, and not from culture.

Fourth, recognize that appearances are not necessarily accurate. When you see someone who has a bigger house or a newer car, they also likely have a bigger mortgage or a larger car payment. They may have toys that you'd love to have, but they may also have a huge home-equity loan to finance all those toys. The stress they may be experiencing from debt may not be readily evident.

And finally, ask for God's help. If you struggle with envy, jealousy or covetousness, ask God to help change your heart and your mind. Usually we have to start by confessing to God and asking for His forgiveness. But then we're able to start with a clean slate that has new possibilities. Ask God to remind you of what you do have when you are tempted to want what someone else has.

FINDING CONTENTMENT

Hearts at Home speaker Karen Ehman says that "contentment isn't having what you want. It's wanting nothing more than what you already have." But the big question we all have is, How do I get to a point where I really don't want more?

The apostle Paul writes in Philippians 4:11–13: "Actually, I don't have a sense of needing anything personally. I've learned by now to be quite content whatever my circumstances. I'm just as happy with little as with much, with much as with little. I've found the recipe for being happy whether full or hungry, hands full or hands empty. Whatever I have, wherever I am, I can make it through anything in the One who makes me who I am." (*The Message*)

What we need to notice in Paul's message is that he speaks of contentment as something to be learned. Contentment isn't something we're born with. It's a character trait that's acquired.

I (Mark) easily admit that this chapter is a tough one for me, and I'm still learning about contentment. My tendency is not to be satisfied with what I have. I am continually drawn in by the want of more. Because I can convince myself why anything more would make my life easier—allowing me to justify purchasing it—I have had to learn to practice the discipline of contentment. With that in mind let's look at eight contentment principles:

1. live beyond the temporary

When we say yes to God and begin a relationship with Him, He wants us to learn to see things in light of eternity. We're designed to live in relationship with God through eternity. This earth is just a stopping point along a far grander journey than we can imagine. The things of this earth are just temporary as well. We can't take any of it with us. We're reminded of this in Matthew 6:20 (NIV): "But store up for yourselves treasures in heaven, where moth and rust do not destroy, and where thieves do not break in and steal."

2. move from own to loan

There isn't anything we have that God hasn't given to us. God owns it all; He's just lending some of it to us. He asks us to be good stewards—or caregivers—of what He has lent to us while we live on this earth. Psalm 24:1 (NIV) tells us, "The earth is the Lord's, and everything in it, the world, and all who live in it."

The word "stewardship" refers to managing someone else's property. Since everything belongs to God, we need to have the attitude that our things are His things, including property, money, relationships, time, talents and even our very lives. In fact, we all have stuff that we can share with others. But some of us struggle to do that. The common fear is that we won't get something back. I (Mark) lend a lot of things out and I have rarely had this happen. However, I have had to teach others how to return what they have borrowed. I will sometimes communicate with ideas like this: "Be sure to clean it before you return it. That will keep it from rusting." "I'm glad I have a truck you can borrow. I filled it up for you. All I ask is that you fill the tank after you're done." "If you dull the new blade, all I ask is that you put a new one in before you return it to me." I want others to partner with me in taking care of God's things, and this is one way in which we can both be good stewards.

3. learn to give

God gives to us so that we can also give to others. We do that first by giving a portion back to God through a tithe, which is 10 percent of our income. We've found that technology can help us tithe. Our paychecks are direct-deposited into our bank account every other Wednesday. Using online banking, we set up an automatic payment of 10 percent of our income to our church every other Thursday in our pay weeks. This assures us that God will get the first gift from our blessing.

Offerings are what we give to others over and above a tithe. Our family sponsors a Compassion child. That's an offering. When we support someone going on a mission trip, it's an offering. Giving to God and to others expands our heart and helps us to keep our hands open to receive gratefully and give cheerfully.

4. praise God

So many of us sit down at the dinner table and say our mealtime prayer on autopilot. "Thank you, God, for this food. Bless it to the nourishment of our bodies. Amen." What if we paused at each meal and really praised God for all He has given to us? "Lord, you are an incredible Creator. Thank you for the warm sunshine today. We praise you for providing for our family: our home, our neighbors, our jobs, our cars, our clothes and our food. We ask you to help us be good stewards of everything you've asked us to manage and take care of. In Jesus' name, amen."

God is worthy of our praise. He has given us so much. And praising God doesn't have to be limited to mealtime prayers—we can do it throughout our day. We can be driving down the road and marveling at the beautiful sunset and say, "God, wow, you are an incredible Creator! Thank you for that sunset." In fact, it's good for our kids to see us talk to God in a casual, spontaneous way like that. If you're alone, praise can be an inside job—you can marvel at the sunset and praise God without saying a word, because He knows our thoughts and the condition of our heart.

5. *grow a thankful heart*

When Jill saw the advertisement for that Blackbeard Boat cruise in Florida that she just knew our boys would love, she had to focus on what we could provide for them: a week at the beach in her parents' condo. When she salivated over the hot Krispy Kreme donuts, she thanked God that we'd had a healthy breakfast that morning that we all fixed together.

When discontentment creeps in, a sure antidote is to change our focus from what we don't have to what we *do* have. This grows a thankful heart. It fosters a grateful spirit and a desire to praise. Contentment is not the fulfillment of what you want, but the realization of how much you already have.

6. *live within your means*

Our thirteen-year-old son wants you to know that he's the *only* kid in the eighth grade who doesn't have a cell phone. While we know that is not true, we also know that he is indeed in the minority. Our teenagers don't get a cell phone until they start driving. Why do we do that to them when it seems as if every other thirteen-year-old in the world has a cell phone? The biggest reason is because we can't afford it.

Most pieces of furniture in our home are worn-out hand-me-downs from friends and family. Some of it matches and some of it doesn't. We'd love to have new furniture, but we don't because it's not in our budget for this season of life.

It's hard to live within our means when it feels as if everyone else's means are more than ours. But we're not responsible for anyone else. Living within the boundaries of what we have and not extending ourselves beyond them is key to managing wisely what God has given to us. It also helps us keep discontentment at bay by establishing guidelines for what we realistically can and cannot afford.

7. accept your circumstances

Someone once said, "Life isn't about waiting for the storms to pass—it's about learning to dance in the rain." Contentment isn't always about the material things we do or don't have. It's also about our lot in life. Are you going through a challenging season in your job? Thank God for how this will grow your character. Is your marriage in a tough place? Ask God how He wants you to grow up and learn something new. Are you dealing with a loss in your life? Ask God to show you, in time, how you might be able to use your experience to encourage others.

Too many of us keep looking for what tomorrow can bring and in doing so we miss today. Live today fully. Don't wish it away or discount it because it looks different than you thought it would. Thank God for today and ask Him to help you know how to live it to His glory.

8. accept your differences

We don't often think about contentment in the marriage relationship. Can you truly say that you are content with your spouse, or are you always working to change him or her? God has created each of us differently. We think, process, verbalize, filter and live out each of these principles differently. We are all wonderfully incompatible!

Mark and I are opposites in so many ways: He loves mornings and I'm a night owl. He loves spicy foods and I want mild. He loves coffee and I love tea. He's an external processor who wants to talk about things, and I'm an internal processor who likes to think and sometimes forgets to talk. Those differences balance us out in so many ways, but unfortunately we often forget that. We end up trying to change each other because we're not content.

In our marriage, some of our biggest arguments have been about money. We see our needs and wants differently. One of us would rather spend and the other would rather save. But God has given us to one another to balance out the extremes.

Are you frustrated or fascinated by your differences? When we can move from frustration to fascination, we are truly able to celebrate how our spouse is different from us. And that is the first step to accepting those differences and letting them strengthen your relationship rather than tear it apart.

THE FRUITS OF CONTENTMENT

We enjoy planting a small garden each summer. There's nothing better than fresh, homegrown tomatoes, summer squash and zucchini. Each year we prepare the ground, plant the seeds and seedlings, water, fertilize and weed. At the end of the growing season we enjoy the fruits that our plants give us.

Our lives are similar. When we plant contentment in our hearts, water, fertilize it with the contentment principles we just talked about, and weed out the places where discontentment begins to grow, we begin to see fruit in our lives.

In John 15:5 (NIV), Jesus tells us, "I am the vine; you are the branches. If a man remains in me and I in him, he will bear much fruit; apart from me you can do nothing." God wants us to see things in this world His way. He wants us to stay connected to His perspectives. When we do that, we're able to see abundant fruit in our lives—happiness, gratitude, conscientiousness and even freedom. Let's look at each of those briefly.

Happiness has nothing to do with our circumstances or our material things. It has everything to do with our attitude toward it all. If God's in charge of our life and we see things in light of eternity, we'll find we are happy and content no matter what's going on in our life. Happiness is a state of mind and a positive frame of mind that is not necessarily giddy or silly. I (Mark) have found happiness flow through me as a calm reaction to and true acceptance of what life brings our way.

Gratitude comes from a full heart. If life is really about all that God is doing, then our heart should be full of thankfulness and praise. Rather than complaining, we should be thankful for all we've been given. And if our goal is simply to have enough, then our hearts can only be thrilled when we have more than enough. Colossians 3:15 (NIV) tells us, "Let the peace of Christ rule in your hearts...and be thankful."

Conscientiousness comes from an attitude of good stewardship. If we recognize that we are stewards of all that God has given to us, we'll be even more conscious of how we use our time, talents and money. Intentionality will increase and wastefulness will decrease. The Bible reminds us of this in Psalm 24:1 (NIV): "The earth is the LORD's, and everything in it, the world, and all who live in it." Because of this truth, we are called to be conscientious about caring for what God has given us.

Freedom is liberating. If we are truly living within our means, we'll find the financial freedom we all long for—not, perhaps, the kind of financial freedom that the world values, but the sort that God calls us to. In doing so we'll also find that giving is easier. Not only that, but when we have contentment, we'll find that our hearts are free to enjoy what we have and not be bound up in envy, jealousy and greed. Psalm 119:45 (NLT) confirms this: "I will walk in freedom, for I have devoted myself to your commandments."

Father God, I do struggle with wanting things I don't have. Sometimes I perceive that it would make my life easier, but honestly I don't know that my perceptions really are accurate. I want to live with a thankful heart that is satisfied fully with what You have provided. I want to live in the moment, fully present in today rather than wishing for something else tomorrow. Show us how to grow contented hearts. Help us to see what we do have and ignore what we don't have. Show us which contentment principle we need to focus on the most. And thank You for all that You have given us. Please show us how to be good stewards of what You have given to us in this temporary life.

let's talk about it

For me, the biggest takeaway from this chapter is . . .

Of the eight contentment principles shared in this chapter, I would like to focus most on . . .

The fruit of contentment I most long for is . . .

chapter 5

sacrifice: forfeit to win!

Jesus went out as usual to the Mount of Olives, and his disciples followed him. On reaching the place, he said to them, "Pray that you will not fall into temptation." He withdrew about a stone's throw beyond them, knelt down, and prayed, "Father, if you are willing, take this cup from me; yet not my will, but yours be done." An angel from heaven appeared to him and strengthened him. And being in anguish, he prayed more earnestly, and his sweat was like drops of blood falling to the ground.
Luke 22:39–44 (NIV)

THIS PICTURE OF JESUS FACING THE ULTIMATE SACRIFICE—His death on the cross for us—illustrates the challenges of any kind of sacrifice. In everyday language Jesus was saying, "God, this is so hard! If there's any way at all that I don't have to go through this, I'm asking you to make that happen. I'm just being honest with you. But it's your gig, God. If this is what I need to do, then so be it."

Those who sacrifice deny themselves something in order to serve a higher cause. Another way to say it is that when we sacrifice, we surrender something of value for the sake of something—or someone—else. Sacrifice is an important part of marriage. We show our love by submitting our time and sometimes our preferences to one another. Parenting requires sacrifice. You suddenly have someone else to consider in all of your decisions. And while parenting is a lifetime commitment, your primary season of sacrifice will take place during the twenty or so years that your child lives in your home and you are responsible for loving them, caring for them, teaching them and eventually ushering them into adulthood.

Living with less requires sacrifice as well. If I want to do less, I may need to sacrifice a hobby I love. If I'm looking for less stress, it could require me to give up volunteering for my favorite cause. If I'm thinking about living on less money, I may have to sacrifice a career opportunity in order to gain more time with my family.

In this chapter we're going to look at both sides of sacrifice. What are some of the things that parents should be willing to sacrifice to give their families more? We'll call those "constructive sacrifices," because they could be necessary, helpful and beneficial to the family. And what are some of the things we should never sacrifice for our children? We'll call those "destructive sacrifices," because making them would negatively affect our family's life. Exploring those two questions is essential for understanding and evaluating sacrifice in our own life.

CONSTRUCTIVE SACRIFICES

If we wanted to live a life without sacrifice, we should have never signed up to be parents. But for most of us, the introduction of real sacrifice began on the day we said the words "I do." Sacrifice is a part of any true and deep relationship—most of all, marriage. Marriage is the merger of two individual lives into one family unit, and in the process of creating that partnership, both people inevitably must sacrifice something of themselves. It's the give and take that molds us into a family unit defined by love.

Parenting comes with some default sacrifices. These are normal sacrifices that most of us need to make at one time or another. In the same way that we sometimes receive constructive criticism—helpful, needed, lovingly offered—these five constructive sacrifices can be made to benefit the health and wellbeing of the family unit.

constructive sacrifice #1: comfort

What parent wouldn't give up their coat if their child were cold? That kind of sacrifice seems to be a natural default for most parents. But some families choose to go even further in sacrificing comfort.

For several years now, the Springer family has chosen to remain in a small house with a small mortgage. This enables Mom to remain at home and their kids to attend a Christian school. In their case, the whole family has sacrificed comfort—Mom, Dad, six children and two dogs share tight living conditions with three small bedrooms. Yet children rarely see sacrifice the same way we do. Sharing a bedroom with a couple of siblings can be normal for them.

For years Mark sacrificed his comfort by continuing to sleep on the waterbed we'd purchased as newlyweds. This wasn't a sacrifice for Jill, who liked our waterbed. But Mark's back needed more support. Each time we got financially close to being able to buy a new bed, we'd add another kid to the family. Their needs would push Mark's need a little farther down the priority list. It was only when Mark's back turned into a pressing health issue that we moved taking care of his need up the priority list. But taking care of the kids' basic needs was our first concern for that season.

Jill sacrificed comfort many times while holding a sleeping baby, especially when we were away from home. Her back would ache from standing or sitting in one position, just keeping our little one asleep or quiet in a public place. On many nights at home, she would work to calm a months-old child enough for them (and everyone else!) to go back to sleep. Her comfort in those moments was secondary to her child's comfort.

As our kids have aged, we've sat outside in freezing temperatures watching way too many soccer games. We've woken at ungodly times of day to help with a paper route. We've endured fifth-grade band concerts where they should have passed out earplugs with the programs. This kind of discomfort—the sacrifice of our comfort—is a necessary part of parenting.

constructive sacrifice #2: sleep

This sacrifice introduces itself the first night your little one comes into this world. A newborn baby can't go twelve hours without food at night. They have to eat every two to four hours. And if they have to eat that often, then someone has to feed them that often! When Jill was nursing our babies, both of us shared the sleep sacrifice. When they woke up crying, Mark would go in and get them out of the crib, change their diapers and then bring them to Jill to nurse. Mark would crawl back in bed, sleep the twenty minutes while Jill nursed, and then put them back to bed after they finished eating. This seemed to work well for most of our newborn years. But then he's pretty good about falling asleep as soon as his head hits the pillow no matter how often he's awakened.

Once your children are sleeping through the night, the sleep sacrifice continues, but usually not nightly. There's the occasional unwelcome but unavoidable "Mommy, I think I'm gonna get sick," but again we share the sacrifice. Jill cleans up the kid and Mark cleans up the bed, the carpet and whatever else they managed to hit along the way.

And if you're not yet to the teen years, let us prepare you for the sacrifice of sleep during that season! If you've set a midnight curfew, it's wise to be awake at midnight to provide much-needed accountability. One upside is that you'll occasionally end up having some of your best conversations with your teen at these times of the night. Jill remembers one night, about a year ago, when she was waiting up for Erica, our seventeen-year-old daughter, to be home at midnight. Evan, our twenty-one-year-old son, who was just two weeks from his wedding, was living back at home that summer. He and Erica arrived home about the same time, and they were both incredibly talkative. The three of them sat at the island in the kitchen and talked until nearly 2:00 AM! It will always be a special memory for her of a wonderful, spontaneous conversation with two of our young-adult children. On that night, her sacrifice of less sleep netted her more time with our soon-to-be-leaving-the-nest children.

Of course, sacrificing sleep over the long haul can become a destructive sacrifice if we're not careful. When the kids were newborns, Jill learned to nap while the baby napped. During the toddler years, Jill and I alternated as to who got up early to fix the bowl of cereal and play blocks. During the teen years, we've alternated who stays up. And due to changes in the school start time this year, we're all going to bed earlier during the week. The reality is that when sleep has to be sacrificed, habits may have to change to protect our health.

constructive sacrifice #3: hobbies

While parents don't want to lose themselves in the midst of parenting, they may have to make adjustments in their hobbies to better fit the needs and finances of the family. Mark loves to golf, but for many of our child-rearing years, that sport was not in our family budget. Rather than giving up something he enjoyed, he found a less expensive alternative he could also enjoy: disc golf. A small investment of about $20 to buy a set of discs was all it took to play on several free courses in town. He introduced some of the guys at church to disc golf (also called Frisbee golf) and now he has a group of four to six guys who play almost weekly. Disc golf not only fits our family financially, but it also is a better fit for our schedule. Eighteen holes of golf require a commitment of up to four hours, whereas eighteen holes of disc golf take just about an hour and a half. This more easily accommodates the additional family activities that are often on our timetable.

constructive sacrifice #4: entertainment/ recreational activities

Our family went without cable television for nearly seventeen years. For Mark, that wasn't a sacrifice made easily. He loves to sit back and watch TV to relax. Jill can take or leave TV so it wasn't such a big deal for her. Every year, we'd sit down and look at our budget to see if there was any way to fit cable into our monthly expenses. Because we'd chosen to live primarily on one income, the reality of our choices stared us square in the face. We weren't willing to sacrifice what we felt was best for our family so we could have cable television. So once again, we recommitted to the sacrifice so we could continue living out our vision for our family.

Did you used to enjoy going to the movies but find that it's now a rarity? Join the club—it's the same for us! Used to have season tickets to watch your favorite team play? Yep, there are a lot of parents who have given that up too. We haven't given up recreation and entertainment completely; we've just found other, less expensive and less time-consuming recreational and entertain-ment options.

We've needed to sacrifice in our own home in other ways as well. There have been plenty of times when we've received a call from one of our teenagers while they're out with some friends: "Mom, can a bunch of us come over and hang at the house?" Mark and I are often already comfortable in our pajamas and every part of us wants to say, "No, not tonight!" But our commitment to provide a safe place for our kids to hang with their friends takes priority over our comfort. We sacrifice so that we know where our kids are, what they're doing and whom they're hanging out with. As we trudge up the stairs to put our clothes back on so we can greet our unexpected company, we remind ourselves that there will be a time when we'll be able to enjoy a Friday night to ourselves—someday. For now, the sacrifice is worth it. Less private time equals more engagement in our teenagers' lives.

constructive sacrifice #5: career

I gave birth to our second child on the day I was supposed to graduate from college. So much for "Pomp and Circumstance." They mailed me my much-awaited diploma a couple of weeks after the ceremony. But then I faced the reality many moms face: I'd worked hard for my degree, and I wanted to use it. But it wasn't to be. There weren't any teaching jobs available in the little Midwestern town we'd moved to so Mark could get his Bible-college degree. So I stayed home by default. Working a non-salaried job and paying for day care for two children just didn't make any sense.

But the early years of my experience opened my heart to making this a permanent arrangement while we were raising our family. Initially, I grieved the reality of this decision. I'd always pictured myself teaching high school music. I envisioned directing the school musicals, creating elaborate Madrigal Dinners, and helping students prepare for solo and ensemble contests each year. I longed for my own choirs filled with students who experienced pride and accomplishment thanks to their hard work. Knowing this wasn't going to be a part of my life, at least in the near future, made me sad—very sad.

And I can't really say that at the outset I loved being at home. It was hard work. It felt isolating, not to mention never-ending. I had plenty of days when I felt disillusioned, and that caused me to question the decision we had made. It wasn't until I mentally reframed motherhood as a career that I finally turned the corner and overcame both grief and frustration. I wasn't wasting my education. I was just applying my education to a different career choice.

In my twenty-three years at home, I've found that being home has actually afforded me other career opportunities that suit my family better than teaching in the school system. For fifteen years, I gave private piano and voice lessons at my home. This brought in income without my ever needing to leave home. After starting and leading a local moms group that eventually birthed Hearts at Home, the world of speaking and writing opened up to me. Again, this was something I could do on my time, in my home, adjusted to the needs of my family. So while I have grieved not using my degree in the way I had imagined, I've also marveled at the doors God has opened during my season at home.

Motherhood is just as valuable a profession as any other. It deserves my best time, energy and knowledge. And though I've sacrificed my formal teaching career, I've gained so much. It's been so rewarding to watch my older children head into adulthood with the character and skills that Mark and I worked so hard to teach them. Being home hasn't ensured that our kids will turn out just like we envisioned—in fact they usually blaze their own individual trails in some way—but it has given me a front-row seat to the fruits of my labor.

Some parents have sacrificed careers to be home full-time. Annette and Ruben are such a couple. At one time they were both climbing up the corporate ladder as State Farm Insurance employees. This worked well until they added baby Andrea to their family. Both Ruben and Annette continued their uphill career climbs until Ruben came face-to-face with the sacrifice he knew he needed to make: "While we both had opportunities within the company, I knew Annette's possibilities as a Latina in management could be especially valuable for her, the company and our family. I had the opportunity to take a job that required a lot of travel, something I really enjoy. However, it quickly became very clear that we couldn't both be traveling for the company and working a high-profile, high-stress job. Someone had to be the stabilizer at home. We had a child to consider now, and I needed to consider her when it came to my career." It takes a strong man to make a decision like this. Ruben sacrificed his career possibilities so that Andrea would have the family environment she needed.

Constructive sacrifices are a necessary part of living with other people. They help both to improve the family and to develop young people into responsible, contributing adults and citizens. Making those sacrifices will help, not hurt, the family.

DESTRUCTIVE SACRIFICES

Sacrifice may be a part of a parent's job description, but there are three things we should never sacrifice. Doing so could result in more stress, less relational intimacy, and possibly even low self-worth. Because of their ability to damage our lives in some way, we'll call these destructive sacrifices. Whatever we do, we want to make sure we are not sacrificing these three things.

destructive sacrifice #1: relationship with God

When Jesus lived on this earth, He was fully God and fully man. Jill recently explored the human experiences of Jesus in her book *Real Moms...Real Jesus*. Researching and writing that book was incredibly eye-opening for her; she began to realize how much Jesus understands our human experiences because He experienced them as well. We're talking about a God who loved us enough not only to reach down to earth as He did throughout the Old Testament but also to actually come to earth and live among us.

We started this chapter with the sacrifice that Jesus made when He gave His life for you and me. When you and I are facing the decision to sacrifice, it makes sense to talk with a Friend who understands—One who has been there. Faced the music. Wanted to run the other way, but knew He had to walk forward in obedience, entrusting His life to His Father.

Sacrifice is rarely easy. It goes against our self-serving, self-sustaining—Okay, let's get honest—selfish nature. It goes against our culture as well. Our society thrives on convenience, revels in taking the easy road, and loves being served rather than serving. So if we're facing an uphill battle, it only makes sense that we probably can't do it on our own strength. We need strength greater than our own, and there's only one place we'll find that: in Jesus.

Sacrificing your time with God is not very smart if you're trying to serve your family through sacrifice. You need God's wisdom. You need His knowledge and understanding. And you need His strength for the long haul.

Think you're too busy? Too tired? You can't do this parenting thing alone. Download a Bible onto your PDA or your iPod so that you have God's Word wherever you are. Implement the daily Proverbs routine we talked about earlier. Talk to God as you run errands or drive to work. When our kids were small, Jill would keep a Bible in every bathroom for a quick word of Truth during the only sixty seconds of the day she just might have alone. And she learned to talk to God while folding laundry. Parenting is the toughest job out there and over the course of raising a child there will be countless times we won't have a clue as to how to handle a parenting challenge. That's when we need someone far wiser than we are. Talk to God and listen for Him. It's the foundation of everything else in your life.

Sacrifice church to sleep in? Not wise in the grand scheme of things. You need that time each week to get realigned to the truth. And you need to be with others who can support you, pray for you and encourage you. Staying connected to other followers of Christ can help you stay strong and headed in the right direction.

Whatever sacrifices you choose to make, don't ever sacrifice your relationship with God. You need Him more than you realize. And He longs for that relationship with you.

destructive sacrifice #2: marriage

"What was it the speaker said about marriage?" Jill asked a friend after a powerful morning listening to a speaker at her moms group. She'd missed part of the speaker's message when she left to change our newborn's diaper.

"Wife first, mother second," she replied. "That seems so hard to do."

Jill had to agree. With three children under seven, motherhood was sucking the life out of her. And it was sucking the life out of our marriage too. We seemed to talk only about diapers and dishes. We rarely left our children to spend any quality time together. We'd become more like roommates than husband and wife. Maybe this speaker was actually on to something.

There's no denying that our children need us. The physical need is very demanding in the early years. They depend on us to feed them, dress them and get them from one point to another. During that season it becomes very easy to look at your spouse and say to yourself, "Okay, you can feed yourself, dress yourself and get yourself wherever you need to go. You're on the bottom of the priority list." Without realizing it, we move our marriage from the front burner to the back burner. It can survive there for a little while, simmering, just keeping warm. But if it sits there untended for too long, the flame will begin to flicker and eventually it will go out. And then it will seem as if we made a wedding vow that said, "I promise to love, honor and cherish you, until *children* do us part."

The best parenting strategy—the one that will benefit your children the most—is to make your marriage a priority. Sure, the temptation is there to say, "Hey, we've only got a short season with our kids. There'll be plenty of time for us after the kids are grown and gone." But the truth is, your kids need you to make your relationship a priority now. Why?

First, it sets a healthy example for their lives and future marriages. Second, it gives your kids the security they long for. When Mom and Dad love each other, their world is okay. And third, your marriage can't survive backburner status. A healthy marriage has to be nurtured and invested in along the way. This keeps the love ignited, the trust strong, the communication open, and the intimacy alive.

Whatever you choose to sacrifice for your children, make sure your marriage isn't on the list.

destructive sacrifice #3: identity

We were sitting in a crowded restaurant one day when our preschool son loudly announced that he had farted. He said it so loudly most people stopped their conversations and turned to look at us.

Jill remembers wanting to crawl under the table.

Later, she thought through why she had been so horrified at his crude announcement, and God's still, small voice of truth lovingly and gently showed her the error of her ways. She was tying her identity to our children's behavior. If our children behaved well, she felt good about herself. If they behaved poorly, she felt bad about herself. What a yo-yo experience! She could be up and down more than a dozen times a day!

We've discovered that this is a common experience for many of us. What is it that *you* unknowingly use to define yourself? Your job? Your title? Your house? The prestige of the neighborhood you live in? Your weight? The color of your teenager's hair? Your children's accomplishments? Your economic status? Marital status? Your clothes? The list goes on and on.

We are all trying to prove we belong somewhere.

In the Book of Matthew, Jesus tells a story about the wise man and the foolish man. The wise man built his house upon a rock. When the rain and winds came, the house stood firm. The foolish man built his house upon the sand. And when the rain and winds came, the house fell with a crash! Jesus isn't talking about house construction—He's talking about life construction. Identity. Having a firm foundation in the things of heaven instead of the things of this world.

When we define ourselves by things such as our job, our economic status, our weight, or our children's behavior, it's like building our lives on sinking sand. The storms of life will blow and we'll crash with our defective, weak foundation. But when we define ourselves based upon how God sees us, then we are building our lives on solid bedrock. God is the same yesterday, today, and tomorrow. He never changes. Because of that, our identities never change.

Parenthood will tempt us to redefine ourselves. We'll work so hard to help our kids that we'll unknowingly sacrifice our own identities on the altar of their success or failure. But doing so will hurt our families. We need to define ourselves by the only thing that never changes in this world: Jesus Christ.

In our busy lives, it's easy to sacrifice our time with God, our marriage and even our identity. But these destructive sacrifices do not help us achieve our vision. Furthermore, they hurt not just us but also our families.

Let's commit today to making the constructive sacrifices we need to make, while protecting the areas of our life that we need never to forfeit. This will give us the necessary balance in sacrifice as we redefine our familial priorities.

Father, thank You for the example of sacrifice You gave us.
Thank You, Jesus, for going to the cross for us. I pray that
You will give me strength to know what a "constructive
sacrifice" is and what a "destructive sacrifice" is. Help me to
have an obedient heart that allows You to lead, even if the
sacrifice will hurt in some way. I also pray for strength, Lord.
Keep me wise and strong, so that time with You is never
sacrificed, nor are my marriage relationship and my identity.
I understand that they are fundamental to my being an
effective parent. Thank You for how You are strengthening
my vision for our family. In Jesus' name, amen.

let's talk about it

After reading this chapter, I've really been thinking about . . .

When it comes to constructive sacrifices, I think we've done well sacrificing . . .

When it comes to destructive sacrifices, I'm concerned that we have sacrificed . . .

chapter 6

simplicity: sometimes less really is more

IT WAS AMERICAN AUTHOR HENRY DAVID THOREAU who, in the mid-1800s, said, "Our lives are frittered away by detail; simplify, simplify." Can you imagine what Thoreau might say today in our consumerist, stressed out, technology-driven culture? Seriously, the environment that we live in promotes *complicating* life rather than *simplifying* it. Fundamentally, we have to understand that, because in this chapter we're going to challenge you to live counterculturally. To swim upstream. To do exactly the opposite of most everyone else. Writing this chapter was challenging for us personally, because even though we've simplified many areas of our lives, we realize that there's so much more to consider!

Simple living is not about existing in poverty or self-inflicted deprivation. Rather, it is about living an examined life—one in which you have determined what is important, or "enough," for you and your family, and then discarded the rest.[3] Often we don't take the time to really inspect our hearts and our habits in order to keep the main thing the main thing.

In this chapter we will identify the main thing by looking at the two parts of simplicity: the inward and the outward. Understanding these two elements can help shift our frame of mind. After you read this chapter, you'll want to get a date night on the calendar with your spouse to talk about what you are learning, how you are being

[3] www.simpleliving.net/main

challenged, and how God is clarifying your vision you to keep home
and family at the top of the priority list.

INWARD SIMPLICITY

We mentioned earlier that over the past year, we've been making
some big transitions in our lives. Mark moved from senior pastor to teaching pastor at the church we planted. Months after
that transition, we felt that God wasn't done. The initial transition was the right step, but just that... a step. With fear and
excitement, Mark has now resigned from his job at the church and
we are committed to encouraging families together through Hearts
at Home. Because Hearts at Home does not yet have the finances
to support full-time employees, we have to raise our own support
and become "domestic missionaries." Leaving church ministry for
Hearts at Home has felt like a very complex decision.

Then we read about inner simplicity in Richard Foster's
book *Celebration of Discipline*: "Simplicity is freedom. Duplicity is
bondage. Simplicity brings joy and balance. Duplicity brings anxiety
and fear."[4] Duplicity happens when we are double-minded. Foster
explains, "One moment we make decisions on the basis of sound
reason and the next moment out of fear of what others will think of
us. We have no unity or focus around which our lives are oriented."[5]

Simplicity is being single-minded—focused only on one thing.
Inward simplicity, in its purest form, comes from keeping Jesus at
the core of our lives. When we were able to peel away the duplicity—
in our case, the pressure to stay in church ministry—we were able to
see the decision we needed to make. We were no longer confused.

[4] Richard Foster, *Celebration of Discipline* (New York: HarperCollins, 1998),
79.
[5] Ibid., 80.

The only question on the table was, "What does God want us to do?" And, because of all the open ministry doors and confirmations through His Word and His people, the answer to that question was clear: "God wants us to move from local church ministry to global family ministry."

God had been showing us that a ministry transition was in our future in so many ways over the past few years. When I moved from duplicity to simplicity, the bondage, anxiety and fear were replaced with freedom, joy and balance. Jesus tells us,

> If you decide for God, living a life of God-worship, it follows that you don't fuss about what's on the table at mealtimes or whether the clothes in your closet are in fashion. There is far more to your life than the food you put in your stomach, more to your outer appearance than the clothes you hang on your body. Look at the birds, free and unfettered, not tied down to a job description, careless in the care of God. And you count far more to him than birds.
>
> Has anyone by fussing in front of the mirror ever gotten taller by so much as an inch? All this time and money wasted on fashion—do you think it makes that much difference? Instead of looking at the fashions, walk out into the fields and look at the wildflowers. They never primp or shop, but have you ever seen color and design quite like it? The ten best-dressed men and women in the country look shabby alongside them.
>
> If God gives such attention to the appearance of wild-flowers—most of which are never even seen—don't you think he'll attend to you, take pride in you, do his best for you? What I'm trying to do here is to get you to relax,

to not be so preoccupied with *getting,* so you can respond to God's *giving.* People who don't know God and the way he works fuss over these things, but you know both God and how he works. Steep your life in God-reality, God-initiative, God-provisions. Don't worry about missing out. You'll find all your everyday human concerns will be met. Matthew 6:25–33 (*The Message*)

We love the way the above verse reads in *The Message* translation of the Bible. It puts things in words that are relevant to our lives. The New Century Version clarifies the main thing even more: "Seek first God's kingdom and what God wants. Then all your other needs will be met as well." Examining our heart and keeping it fully focused on God is what inner simplicity is all about.

TRUST

Inner simplicity is really about trust. Do I trust that God is in charge of my life? Do I trust Him to have my best interests in mind? Do I trust Him even when it doesn't make sense? Coming to grips with the answers to these questions moves us from trust to faith, which we'll explore more fully in Chapter 8.

Richard Foster identifies three inner attitudes that are essential to inner simplicity. Let's explore each one and apply it to our lives.

The first attitude is that we have to view what we have as a gift from God. What we have is not the result of our efforts. This is hard for us to fathom in our "self-made" world, but we really are dependent on God for everything. During the recent economic crisis, many people have found this to be true. Hard-working employees who have given much of their lives to a company have found themselves without a job when the company went under. God, they've discovered, is our only provider. Do you live with an attitude that reflects your knowledge and acceptance of this truth? Once we got our focus on God as our Provider, it cleared out the confusion in both of our minds about our ministry transition.

The second attitude Foster outlines is that we must understand that it's God's job to take care of what we have. This doesn't mean we can be irresponsible and throw caution to the wind. He still wants us to be good stewards, good caretakers, of what He has given us. But there is a sense of freedom in knowing that we can trust God to take care of us and of our families. We can't be with our children all the time, but God can. He is our protector. How are you doing simply believing that God is the ultimate protector? Once reminded of this truth, we stopped worrying about how our transition might affect our boys. We trust that God is bigger than that challenge.

The third attitude is one of generosity: Our possessions are available to others. Since they really don't belong to us, then we are free to share them. Whether money, things or time, it's all God's to use as He needs. This is challenging for us to do because we tend to be self-centered and self-focused rather than God-focused. What would happen if we got up every morning and said, "God, you've given me so much. Please show me how to use my money, my possessions and my time for your purposes today."? If we prayed that each morning—really meant it—we'd probably be more likely to see God work through our lives.

When we "seek first the kingdom of God," we experience real inner simplicity. No chaos. No confusion. Just vision to live our lives with one singular focus on God. And that inner simplicity *will* equip us to live our less-is-more lives.

OUTWARD SIMPLICITY

Once we have experienced inward simplicity, outward simplicity will follow.

Any effort to start with outward simplicity will lead to short-lived results, because our hearts guide our habits. In fact, if we try to focus on outward simplicity first, we'll run the risk of legalism—focusing on rules rather than relationships. If we start with the relationship piece, we can then experience the release of outward simplicity!

Foster explores ten controlling principles for the outward expression of simplicity.[6] These are not rules, but guidelines to help us experience outward simplicity. As we survey them, take the time to examine your heart and habits and think about how they are defining your family's priorities.

First, buy things for their usefulness rather than for their status. Think about housing, transportation, furniture and clothes. Rather than asking, "What do I want?" you should be asking, "What do I really need?" Resist the urge to impress people with your stuff. Be more concerned with how you live your life, your integrity and your character.

Second, reject anything that is addictive to you. If anything controls us, it becomes an idol—or a god—to us. The first of the Ten Commandments is "you shall have no other gods before me." (Exodus 20:3) Anything that controls us is a god to us. Refuse to be controlled by anything other than the one true God.

Third, get in the habit of giving things away. This habit helps us loosen our grip on our possessions. It reminds us that it all belongs to God anyway. A good strategy for giving things away is to de-clutter your home regularly. Most of us could give away half of what we own and never really miss much!

Fourth, refuse to believe that you need the newest and the best. It's almost impossible to own something these days that isn't outdated within a matter of a few months. A newer version always has

[6] Adapted from Foster, 90–95.

better technology, better features, or better value. Too often "new" seduces us to buy something we really don't need. A less-is-more mindset isn't excited about the new offerings if what we have works just fine.

Fifth, learn to enjoy things without owning them. Enjoy community to the fullest by tapping into shared resources such as city parks, public beaches and the local library. The less we own, the less we have to manage. And we'll find more time for relationships when we have to care for fewer things.

Sixth, develop a deeper appreciation for creation. Take time to enjoy the beauty of the earth and the animals that God created. Gaze at a beautiful sunset. Watch a butterfly move from flower to flower. Walk through the grass barefoot. Marvel at the intricate designs of different flowers and while you're at it, enjoy the beautiful smells God has given to each one.

Seventh, become skeptical of "buy now, pay later" schemes. We'll talk about these more in Part III, but the general concept here is that debt puts us in bondage. Simplicity is freedom, not bondage. Less debt means more freedom.

Eighth, obey Jesus' instructions about plain, honest speech. Jesus tells us in Matthew 5:33–37 (*The Message*), "And don't say anything you don't mean.... You only make things worse when you lay down a smoke screen of pious talk, saying, 'I'll pray for you,' and never doing it, or saying, 'God be with you,' and not meaning it. You don't make your words true by embellishing them with religious lace. In making your speech sound more religious, it becomes less true. Just say 'yes' and 'no.' When you manipulate words to get your own way, you go wrong." We say things we don't mean when we move away from the main thing, which is our sole focus on God. If God is controlling our tongue, the result will be sincere words.

Ninth, reject anything that oppresses others. This is one we're still working on. It has only been in the past few years that we've considered how the products we use are actually made. We're beginning to check labels, look for where items are made, and select products that are labeled with the words "fair trade." While we're not to the place of being able to always purchase fair-trade products—they typically cost more—we're certainly paying attention more than we have in the past. We realize that if our lust for wealth or certain products means the poverty of others, then we should be saying, "No, thanks." We have to resist the temptation to buy by convenience or price and instead purchase with integrity.

Tenth, turn away from anything that distracts you from seeking the kingdom of God first. What is the center of attention in your life? Even family can distract us from the main thing. We certainly shouldn't "turn away" from family, but we do need to get it in its rightful place in our lives. Put God first, and the rest will fall into place.

DOWNSIZING IS REALLY UPSIZING

So what is it that's complicating your life the most? Where do you have confusion rather than clarity? Where are you bound up rather than free? Rather than resigning yourself to the stress, the crazy schedule, and the splintered family, consider how your heart and your habits can benefit from inward and outward simplification. You see, downsizing some parts of life just might mean upsizing others for your family. E. F. Schumacher, an economic thinker, put it best by saying, "Any intelligent fool can make things bigger, more complex, and more violent. It takes a touch of genius—and a lot of courage—to move in the opposite direction."

Because we are created in the image of God, our hearts long for the things of God. When we are able to put first things first, we find the simplicity we've actually been longing for. When we pursue living with less, part of the more we find is more of God. And that's a "more" we desperately need.

Lord, help us to see life differently. Give us the courage to change what we can change. Help us to honestly evaluate our hearts and our habits to determine if they are helping us accomplish what we want to accomplish in our marriage and family. We can't do this without You, Lord. We need Your wisdom, Your strength and Your help to swim upstream, if that's what You are laying on our hearts to do.
In Jesus' name, amen.

let's talk about it

The biggest takeaway that I have from this chapter is . . .

When thinking about inward simplicity, what I struggle with the most is . . .

Of the ten principles of outward simplicity, I feel most challenged and convicted to . . .

chapter 7

frugality: living with more time and less money

ONE EVENING MORE THAN TWENTY YEARS AGO, we sat at the dining-room table discussing our monthly budget. Money was tight as usual. Living on less requires regular conversations about strategy and this was one such talk. "We have to get in our mind that we have more time than money," one of us stated. That statement proved to be foundational in our thinking. In fact, changing our thinking about our balance of time and money was the first step in making right decisions about our expenses.

We still have those conversations. And honestly, our thinking has to be refreshed quite often because convenience can so easily overshadow frugality, especially on a day when your body is tired and your resolve is weak.

We revisited this recently when we were getting ready to leave for vacation. I (Mark) went to get the oil changed and the tires rotated. We had coupons for a free oil change at a dealership and a warranty for a free tire rotation at Walmart. The oil change took almost an hour, and I began to rationalize just having the tires rotated at the dealership. Walmart could take one or two hours for the tire rotation, and I didn't want to spend my whole day waiting in auto shops. I decided that we had too much to do so I asked the shop to go ahead and rotate the tires ($20) and change the wiper blade on our back window ($18). By the time I left, our "free" oil change and the conveniences I had rationalized had cost us nearly $40. My dear, frustrated wife reminded me that $40 is almost a full tank of gas. Amazingly, I had not thought of that! Nor had I thought through all of my options. We lived less than three miles from Walmart. I could have dropped off the vehicle for the tire rotation and had Jill or one of my teenagers come pick me up. I didn't need to spend my whole day waiting in an auto shop, as I'd rationalized. I could have gotten all the work done for about $8—which is what my total outlay would have been if I'd purchased the windshield wiper for the back window and done the labor myself. I lost my long-term vision for short-term convenience.

If a family chooses to live with less money, both partners need to buy into the concept of frugality. If one parent comes home for a season, part of that parent's job description can be to make sure the family lives as frugally as possible. Sometimes, you can find the equivalent of a second income from saving money rather than making money! Understanding that finding ways to save money wherever possible is actually part of the job of being at home is key to being a successfully thrifty family.

We have found that frugal families share several habits that help make them successful. Let's explore eight Thrifty Thoughts that frugal families have in common.

THRIFTY THOUGHT #1: APPRECIATE

Have you ever known people who, even though they have all they need, still want more? There's an initial excitement whenever they acquire something new, but that wears off quickly, and then the hunt for a new high begins again. You may find that this actually describes you. This person has likely developed an inability to appreciate.

Every new toy, new piece of clothing, new tool and new kitchen gadget is fun for the moment. Over time, however, it all falls into one big category labeled "stuff." No special memories. Nothing stands out. It's just all stuff. And none of it is really special—because there's just too much for any of it to be special.

Our sense of appreciation becomes dulled. Because we give in to our wants and we rarely deprive ourselves, we might miss out on the simple pleasures in life. Sometimes it can happen when we miss out on the joys of doing something that we are accustomed to outsourcing. For instance, if you eat out more often than you eat at home, you miss out on the specialness of eating out and appreciating what it takes to make a great-tasting meal. And you miss out on really appreciating the art of cooking. Sure, not all of us will enjoy cooking. Honestly, Jill would rather do anything else but cook. However, she's learning to appreciate the nuances of new seasonings, and has recently taken on the challenge of learning to cook tasty meals that are low in sodium and low-calorie, due to health factors in our family. Sometimes a new interest or a new hobby can increase our sense of appreciation.

THRIFTY THOUGHT #2: RESEARCH

Thrifty families take time to research their purchases. They are so careful about spending money that they want to make sure they are getting the best deal and using their limited income wisely. When considering a purchase you can:

- Comparison-shop with print ads so you can find the best prices being offered. Many stores will match prices if you can produce an ad from one of their competitors. This is especially helpful with food as well as health and beauty aids you buy regularly. There's no need to go from store to store to get the best deals. Go to your favorite store with your proof of prices in hand and ask them to match the printed price. Most grocery stores will do this. It takes time to look through the ads, but in this case, time is money that stays in your pocket!

- Ask friends and family about their past purchases. Most of us have a good-sized network at our fingertips that we rarely use to the fullest. If you need to buy a new appliance, send out an e-mail asking friends and family if they have any recommendations of brand, style or store. We recently did this when another dishwasher died (we seem to have a problem with dishwashers, don't we?), and to our surprise, a friend of ours knew someone who had replaced a dishwasher for aesthetic reasons. It worked fine, but didn't have the look they wanted in their remodeled kitchen. They just wanted to get rid of it, so they agreed to give it to us if we'd come pick it up! Personally, we didn't care what color it was—we just wanted something that worked. It was a win-win for both of us.

- Use the Internet. The Web is amazing—never has research been more available, right at our fingertips! If you are thinking about making a purchase, look online for customer reviews of the products you are considering. While we both hate to purchase an online subscription to anything, we've found great value in subscribing to *Consumer Reports* online. Jill's dad has subscribed to the *Consumer Reports* print magazine for years. We prefer the online version so that we don't have magazines piling up around the house. Their unbiased testing has been extremely helpful in making wise purchases over the years.

- Interview your family members. Who will be using this item you are purchasing? What are their needs or expectations? What do they hope to do with the purchase? Do they have any insight or perspective you need to consider? Asking these kinds of questions is helpful in making an informed decision that is wise for all involved.

- Consider a previously owned product. Depending on what you are looking for, eBay, Craigslist, and freecycle.com are great places to find new or gently used products at a discount.

- Shop a couple of different stores for the same product to get accurate and consistent information about the product. This expands your knowledge of the product and is research from a slightly different angle, but it can be very helpful in making a wise purchase.

- Resist rushing big-ticket buying decisions. A wait can give us time to research, and it can also help us evaluate if we actually need to make the purchase or if we might even consider doing without.

THRIFTY THOUGHT #3: ORGANIZE

There is a lot of advertising streaming into our homes: newspaper ads, coupon booklets, online coupons, discount codes, coupon post-cards and more. Having an organization system for all of these discount deals can save you a ton of money! Here are some suggestions from frugal families who make organization a priority:

- Make a list of all the restaurants in town that offer free children's meals on a designated day each week. Design the list so it is categorized by the day when the offer is valid. This allows for a quick peek at the list to determine what restaurant might be the most affordable for your family to eat at.

- Save the weekly grocery-store ads in a folder in your car. If you go to the grocery store you'll be armed with the deals of the week and you can ask the store to match its competitors' sale prices.

- Organize restaurant and clothing-store coupons in alphabetical order and by expiration date. Carry the coupons with you in your car or purse. A coupon organizer works well for some and an 8 $^1/_2''$ × 11″ three-ring binder for others. The important thing is that you use a system that works for you.

- Create a "home" for you to compile coupons in each week. Once a week, sit down and cut out and organize your coupons using whatever coupon organizer system you devise. The key is to establish a routine.

THRIFTY THOUGHT #4: SWAP

Our country has a long tradition of bartering. Doctors used to be paid with fresh chickens and produce; farmhands were provided free room and board. In today's culture, we seem to have lost the fine art of bartering, but in the current economic stress, we're seeing more families revisit the concept.

Our family bartered childcare services for years to allow us an inexpensive, consistent date night. We found a family with similar parenting styles and children of like ages, and set up a regular schedule of swapping childcare services. Our kids loved playing with their friends, and we loved the time for just the two of us. Even on the nights that we did the babysitting, we found our children played so well together that we actually had a bit of a break ourselves.

During the kids' preschool years, Jill traded "days off" with a girlfriend. Every Tuesday was our trade day. One week was Jill's day off, and Sue would watch our kids. The next week was Sue's day off, and Jill took care of her kids. Neither spent a dime to make it happen, but both reaped the benefits of the exchange.

What talents do you have to offer to someone else? When we wanted our son to receive extra tutoring at a local learning center, we could hardly afford the $250-per-month price tag. After Jill learned that the director of the center was writing a book on learning challenges, she offered her publishing experience and editing services in exchange for a lower monthly fee. The director was willing to make the trade, and we both benefited from the arrangement.

Many times we're afraid to ask for these kinds of arrangements. But in today's economic climate, the thrifty parent needs to consider all options to make sure there's actually money in the bank at the end of the month! And with so many home businesses out there, the possibilities of bartering are even better. When Jill was teaching piano and giving voice lessons, she would have gladly bartered guitar lessons for one of our children and art lessons for another.

THRIFTY THOUGHT #5: QUESTION

When considering a purchase, the frugal family is willing to ask themselves two tough questions. The first is, "Do we really need this?" The second: "Is there any other option for us?"

About fifteen years ago, we were once again faced with a broken dishwasher. When we looked at our financial picture, we realized that purchasing a dishwasher would have required us to go into debt. That was something we were trying hard not to do. So we asked ourselves, "Do we really need this?"

The answer to that was "no." A family can live without a dishwasher. We'd certainly love to have one, but we don't absolutely need one. Then we asked, "Is there any other option for us?"

The answer to that was "yes." We actually had three dishwashers in our house, and they even had names: Anne, Evan and Erica. While Mark and I had been without a dishwasher early in our marriage, our kids had never had to wash dishes by hand. We decided it could be valuable for us to provide them with this experience. Remember the concept of appreciation? After nine months of washing dishes by hand, we all had a special appreciation for the new—to us…it was actually used!—dishwasher we finally found. We also found that we had some wonderful one-on-one time with one of our kids each night after dinner as we washed and dried the dishes together. It wasn't ideal, but it was the best financial decision for us at the time.

Another thing we can question is why we need all the fancy toys that are available for our children these days. Have you ever noticed how a young child is often far more interested in the box that a toy came in rather than in the toy itself? Why don't we get the hint? Children really don't need fancy toys. A few well-chosen everyday items can go a long way in keeping a child busy. Got any of these around the house?

- Laundry basket
- Blanket
- Pots and pans
- Wooden spoons
- Rice
- Kitchen funnel
- Boxes of various shapes and sizes
- Chocolate pudding (great for finger painting)
- Balls
- Hats
- Old clothes for dressing up
- Old socks (make great hand puppets)

If you have these items, you have just about everything a kid needs in the first few years of life! Sure it's nice to have a few toys, but it's not as necessary as we're led to believe. Simple is just as effective and a lot less expensive. The frugal family questions the status quo and decides to do things differently.

THRIFTY THOUGHT #6: MANAGE

The frugal family knows what stuff they have and where it is. They understand that both time and money can be wasted by having to manage too much stuff. When it comes to material things, the less we have, the less we have to manage, clean and organize.

Jill used to be amazed at one particular friend's home. It was always neat and tidy. One day she looked closer and noticed that it wasn't especially clean, but you really didn't see that because it was well-organized. And when she carefully evaluated her neat home and our messy one, she came to realize what really made the difference: Her friend had less stuff than we did!

Over the years we've learned to simplify a lot in the "stuff" category. We still have a long way to go, but we've found a few strategies that make a huge difference.

- Give it away. When you are de-cluttering, get it out of your house the very same day if you can. Donate it to Goodwill or your local mission. Make sure to keep a list of what you're donating and get a receipt so that you can take a deduction on your taxes for a charitable contribution. Put a DONATE box—we use an extra laundry basket—on each level of your home so you'll have a place to put items or clothing you discover you have but don't need anymore.
- Give everything a home. When I start seeing piles on my kitchen counter, I realize that I am either not using the "homes" I have established for things or that I need to establish new homes. Recently I noticed that I was piling up ads and coupons I'd pulled out of the paper but hadn't had time to peruse and cut out. I realized that I needed to create a home for these things, and the kitchen counter wasn't an option. I created a hanging folder for the coupons and ads and put it in a file cabinet. Now those items have a permanent home and I know where to find them when I need them.

Manage how much stuff is actually coming into the house with these strategies:

- Don't watch commercials on television. The less you are exposed to commercials, the less you are tempted to buy things you don't really need. If you have a DVR, use it to weed out the commercials. A one-hour show usually has twenty minutes of commercials.
- Don't go to the mall or a store without a purpose in mind. Window-shopping can cost a lot of money and bust the budget before you know it.
- Don't look at catalogs unless you need something specific. In fact, call the catalog companies and ask them to remove you from their mailing lists. Everything in the catalog is on the Internet anyway, so if you need something, you can still find it.
- Don't buy anything unless you've decided in advance where it will live in your home. If our kids have heard us say it once, they've heard it a million times when we are picking up: "Everything in its home, please." Thinking about its "home" before you purchase it just might cause you to decide that you don't really need it.
- Resist bringing things home just because they are free. Every year our family hits the county fair. One stroll through the exhibit area nets an armful of free items. But clutter isn't freeing: it's constricting. So these items really aren't free then, are they? They cost you stress. Don't hesitate to say no or stop by the trash can on the way out the door.
- Stop the junk mail! Contact the Direct Marketing Association and ask them to remove you from their mailing list. This will keep them from selling your name and address to other companies. Also don't fall for sweepstakes gimmicks and drawings. These are designed to secure your address for future advertising. If you don't fill out the forms, they won't get your address.

THRIFTY THOUGHT #7: REDEFINE

Thrifty families watch out for luxuries dressed up as necessities. Rather than assuming they need something, they ask themselves if there are other options. One of Jill's favorite "frugal" bloggers is Crystal, who writes on the Money-Saving Mom (www.moneysavingmom.com) blog. Her favorite post is one where Crystal talks about redefining paper towels from a necessity to a luxury. Here's how she describes that decision:

You want to know how we've eliminated paper towels from our home? Well, here's the answer: *I just stopped buying them.* Seriously, that was it.

About two years ago or so, I realized that paper towels were one item I could never find that great of a deal on and I most assuredly never seemed to be able to snag them for free. I also realized that these were an item many people lived without for thousands of years, without being the worse for it.

So I talked to my husband and asked him if I could do an experiment: Could I just stop buying paper towels and see if we missed them?

You know what? We never really even noticed. When we needed to clean up a spill, we just used a towel. When we needed to wipe something up, we used a rag. And so on. I keep a drawer-full of towels and rags in the kitchen handy for these types of things.

Honestly, the only times I've realized we didn't have paper towels were when someone was at our home and they asked for a paper towel. I'd just tell them we actually don't use paper towels, but the rags or towels are in the bottom drawer in the kitchen.

We've received quite a few reactions of shock to that statement. It seems as if the thought of living without paper towels is a pretty foreign idea to most Americans. . . . Now, I'm not writing this to make the case that all of you need to quit buying paper towels. However, I share it as an example of how there are many things we've come to think are "necessities" in life which really aren't.[7]

I love Crystal's challenge! What if we evaluated our "necessities" more often to see if they really might be luxuries dressed up as necessities? Some of us are already doing this. Have you determined that water bottles are not a necessity? A travel mug or reusable water bottle that we fill from the tap works just fine. Another family we know has determined that they won't purchase expensive cleaning products. They make their own by mixing lemon-scented ammonia with water in a spray bottle. This kind of thinking is a huge strategy in living a less-is-more lifestyle.

THRIFTY THOUGHT #8: GENERATE

The frugal family values creativity and generates ideas rather than accepting the usual way of doing things. Lisa, a mom of two boys ages five and seven, posted on her well-known blog, Stretch Mark Mama (www.stretchmarkmama.blogspot.com), that she had taught her kids how to play "Coins in a Bucket" one summer afternoon. She took a five-gallon bucket, filled it with water, and tossed a quarter in the bottom. She then gave her boys a handful of pennies and they each took turns dropping pennies one at a time into the water. The first penny to land on the quarter is the winner. Talk about simple! A bucket + water + a quarter + a few pennies = hours of fun. And the best part, she said, was digging the pennies out of the water to cool the boys down on a hot day. Now that's some frugal family entertainment!

One winter day we sent our boys outside with a bottle of bubbles and a bubble wand in their gloved hands. Do you know what

---

[7] www.moneysavingmom.com/money_saving_mom/2009/03/is-it-really-a-necessity.html

happens to bubbles when the temperature is below freezing? They freeze like glass balls and provide great entertainment for even a preteen!

Who says that having fun has to cost money? Too many of us default to thinking that the best entertainment is found at the movie theater, an expensive theme park or a major-league ballpark. While those kinds of activities are enjoyable on occasion, the family that's looking for frugal fun can find it right at home with a little bit of inspiration. Generate some ideas of your own or try these no-cost favorites we often forget about:

- Card games: solitaire, double solitaire, hearts, spades, Go Fish. As the kids grow older, teach them more complicated games like euchre or gin rummy.
- Board games: Monopoly, Candy Land, Scrabble, Life, chess, checkers, Clue.
- Yard games: Tag, hide-and-seek, beanbag toss, water balloons, hopscotch, Frisbee.
- Outdoors: Fishing, hiking, biking, picnic at a park, free concerts in the park, Frisbee golf (free in most cities), scavenger hunts.
- Indoors: Build a fort with blankets and kitchen chairs, make an appliance box into a hideout, read a book aloud as a family or play jacks.

Need some more ideas? Check out www.funattic.com/game_list. It has the most comprehensive list of games and activities we've seen anywhere. Sometimes all we need to do to generate some new ideas is to get the wheels turning in our own head.

The frugal family learns how to think outside the box. They question commonly accepted standards and ask themselves if there is another way of looking at things. Their commitment to frugality over convenience keeps them in the mindset that they just may have more time than money. Rethinking expenses helps us redefine priorities. And that's an important step in becoming a less-is-more family.

Father God, I admit that convenience often trumps frugal finances in my daily life. Give me the energy to put in the extra time to help us spend less money. I also ask that I would be sensitive to hearing Your voice when I want to take the easy but more expensive road. Help me to be a wise steward of what You have given to me to manage. Remake my heart and mind to think "thrifty thoughts" more often. Thank You for leading me and teaching me ways that I can manage Your resources better for Your purposes and our family's needs. In Jesus' name, amen.

let's talk about it

This chapter has made me think about . . .

Of the eight Thrifty Thoughts, I'd love to see us implement these two . . .

My concerns about Thrifty Thinking are . . .

chapter 8

faith: ordinary people trusting in an extraordinary God

THE PHONE RANG THIRTY MINUTES AFTER MARK LEFT FOR WORK. I answered it, and was surprised to hear his voice on the other end of the line. It was Mark's last semester of Bible college, and in addition to attending classes and finishing up an internship, he had a part-time job installing flooring for a local home-decorating store. "Well, I have good news and I have bad news," he began. "The bad news is that I have no job. When I arrived to pick up my jobs this morning, I walked into a liquidation sale. They're closing the store and not one employee knew it until this morning." He continued, "The good news is that everything here is dirt cheap. Is there anything we need for our apartment?"

I was standing in the kitchen of our small home looking out the back patio window when a thought came to mind. "Well, do they happen to have any vertical blinds? These curtains at the back window are looking nasty," I said, referring to the thirty-year-old curtains that had come with the apartment. He responded that he didn't know, but he'd take a look and see.

About an hour later he came home beaming. "Check this out, Jill." He was carrying a big long box. Inside the box was a full set of insulated vertical blinds; they were a dusty rose color that matched our couch and chairs beautifully. "Mark," I gasped, "these are beautiful. How much did you have to pay for them?" He went on to explain that there was not just one set but two, and they had given them to him for $20. Our bedroom had a window that we would be able to cover too. Thank You, God!

But God wasn't done with the surprises just yet. While we were installing the blinds, our neighbor Patty dropped by to see our God-gift! "Boy, I sure do wish I'd known about this deal. We'd love to have some nicer window coverings too," she lamented. As Mark was finishing installing the second set, we noticed there were still quite a few blinds and some hardware in the box. Upon further investigation, we discovered that there were not two sets of blinds in the box but three! As soon as we made that discovery, Patty piped up, "I'll pay you $20 for that set of blinds and I won't take no for an answer!" She dropped a $20 bill in Mark's hand and headed out the door dragging the box of blinds behind her.

Mark and I stood in the living room astonished at God's provision. We were reminded that day that God cares about our needs and our wants. New window coverings were definitely not a need for our family, but God cared about it nonetheless. And He provided them to us at no cost.

Stories like this have been commonplace in our family's journey of faith. Jill shared many of our God stories in her most recent book *Real Moms…Real Jesus*. There's the "Pond God Story," in which God provided all of the elements needed to create a beautiful backyard pond to fill an empty hole in our yard. There's the "Adoption God Story," in which God, in just nine months, provided us the $36,000 needed to adopt our son from Russia. And then there's the "Bread and Milk God Story," in which the nonprofit agency Mark was working for couldn't pay him for three months and God provided bread and milk for three months in one incredible delivery from our neighbor in a pickup truck. We've spent twenty-three years living on less than society has declared a family of our size needs.

But during those years, God has blessed us with more than we could ever have imagined.

However, that faith journey has not always been easy. There have been plenty of times that our fear has seemed bigger than our faith, and the ride has often felt something like a roller coaster. But God has never let us down. When we've allowed Him to lead, it's always been a faith-building experience.

WHO'S IN CONTROL?

It's safe to say that most of us like to have a sense of control over our lives. We like to know what's going to happen, how it's going to affect us, and what we can do about it. And that's exactly why faith is so hard; we are not in control. God is.

The best picture of faith I have ever seen happened in the movie *Indiana Jones and the Last Crusade*. Indiana Jones is on an adventure to find the Holy Grail. He finds himself on the edge of a cliff. It appears that the nothingness in front of him is bottomless. One false step and he's gone forever.

With the bad guys close behind, Indiana Jones stands on the edge of what looks to be a one-foot-wide ledge, with his back plastered against a stone wall. He keeps repeating the instructions he's been given, which indicate that if he takes a step, a bridge will appear. But it appears that he will be stepping off the cliff and causing his own death. He's cloaked in fear like a blanket. Sweat is pouring off his forehead. He finally realizes that he has to follow the instructions, so he places his foot over the nothingness to take the step. As he does so, his foot drops slightly; it appears that there is nothing to catch him. But as he continues, a bridge materializes; he is able to use it to cross to the other side before his pursuers, who are unable to see the bridge, can catch him.

That, friends, is what faith often looks like. It's so scary to trust in a God that we cannot see. The Bible says that "faith is being

sure of what we hope for, and certain of what we do not see."
(Hebrews 11:1) Most of us don't have a problem with being sure
of what we hope for. But certain of what we do not see? That's a
bigger problem! We like to see for ourselves what's up. We want to
know what's going to happen next. And we'd really like to see the
outcome of a situation before we start walking it out. Bottom line:
We want to be in control.

However, if a family chooses to live on less, walking by faith and
letting God be in control is absolutely necessary. The Bible encourages us to walk by faith in James 1:2–8 (*The Message*):

> Consider it a sheer gift, friends, when tests and challenges
> come at you from all sides. You know that under pressure,
> your faith-life is forced into the open and shows its true
> colors. So don't try to get out of anything prematurely. Let it
> do its work so you become mature and well-developed, not
> deficient in any way.
>
> If you don't know what you're doing, pray to the Father. He
> loves to help. You'll get his help, and won't be condescended
> to when you ask for it. Ask boldly, believingly, without a
> second thought. People who "worry their prayers" are like
> wind-whipped waves. Don't think you're going to get any-
> thing from the Master that way, adrift at sea, keeping all your
> options open.

This passage tells us that we need to live this life partnering with
God. Replace worry with prayer. Let challenges strengthen you and
mature you. Trust God to help.

While we work hard to live within our means, there have been
several seasons of our life during which we've had to say, "God,
we've done what we can. We have to trust You for the rest." He's
always provided for us—but not always in the ways we expect
Him to.

Once, when Mark was in Bible college, we needed to pay our electric bill, and we simply didn't have enough income that month to cover all our bills. On the day the electric bill was due, a letter from the hospital where our son Evan had been born a year earlier arrived. The letter explained that while our account was paid in full, we had been overcharged and the hospital owed us a refund. The check enclosed was exactly the amount we needed to pay the electric bill. *God provided with perfect timing.*

A month later we were able to pay all of our bills, but didn't have any more money to go to the grocery store. We were getting creative: We tried to use the remaining items in our cabinets and our freezer to make meals. One morning we awoke to a sack of groceries on our front porch. We weren't the only ones who received that day—seven other apartments in our building had received a sack of groceries sometime in the night. *God provided through His people.*

Several years ago, Mark finally decided to explore hearing loss he'd struggled with for years (and all those years Jill thought he was just ignoring her!). After a visit to the audiologist, it was determined that his hearing loss was so severe that hearing aids were recommended. After he came to terms with needing hearing aids at the age of forty-four, we looked at the costs of getting a pair. We were floored; the $6,000 for the recommended technology was not in our budget at all. But during our discussion with the audiologist, she suggested we contact the Illinois Department of Rehabilitation. Because Mark needed to hear for his job, he might qualify for a full or partial grant to get the hearing aids. We contacted the office, applied for the grant, and several months later Mark received a call that he had qualified for the full grant! Because of our income level, he received his hearing aids with no out-of-pocket expense whatsoever. *God provided through the wisdom and knowledge of others.*

During a month when we'd had more medical expenses than our budget allowed, we found ourselves struggling to have the money for food and gas to finish out the month. Then Mark received a phone call asking him to install a room of carpet. Installing flooring was a job he'd done in the past, but he'd left the business to pursue full-time ministry. He decided to take the job and we were able to pay all our bills that month. *God provided an unexpected job to make ends meet.*

Another time when we'd had some unexpected automobile expenses, we found ourselves with more month at the end of our money. As Jill sat paying the bills one afternoon, she noticed a $10 charge on our phone bill that she'd never noticed before. It didn't seem like an accurate charge, so she called the company and inquired about the bill. After looking at our account, the customer service representative responded, "Mrs. Savage, you are correct. This charge should not be on your bill. However, it appears we've been making the error for over a year now. It looks like we owe you $150. I'll send out that refund right away." *God provided unexpected insight and wisdom to meet our needs.*

Looking at our checkbook one very busy month, Jill found that we had very little money left for gas and food and there were still two weeks left in our monthly budget. A closer look at our spending habits caused her to look at our careless, convenience-inspired spending. We'd gotten lazy, and we had eaten out too many times during the first two weeks of the month. The resulting shortfall was our own fault. She shared her findings with me and our conviction led to a heartfelt apology to God for not being good stewards of our income. We both recommitted to our money plan and the daily decisions we needed to consistently make. We worked together to tighten our belts and figure out a plan for the remaining two weeks of the month. *God provided for us that month with accountability.*

God certainly wants us to be responsible. The Bible, particularly in Proverbs, is full of wisdom about being responsible with money. That is the way we need to live our lives everyday. But sometimes

God asks us to do things that don't make sense. His ways are not our ways. We can't put God in a box labeled "stewardship" at one end of the spectrum and forget about another box labeled "miracles" at the other side of the spectrum. We have to grow our picture of God to include all of who He is. He's not at just the responsibility side of the spectrum or at the miracle side of the spectrum. He inhabits the whole. He is a big God and we have to be open to whatever He asks us to do even if it's on part of the spectrum we are less familiar with.

God rarely does things the way we might expect or even the way we might request it. But He always responds in some way. The more we've walked by faith, the more we've learned that we can trust God. In fact, trust is a by-product of faith. The more we trust, the more we give over the control to the One who can really do something with our life. Living on less has not only given us more for our family, but also allowed us to experience more of God!

TRUST

Following a mission trip to Haiti, our friend Michele Cushatt shared some powerful thoughts on her blog about trusting God. Her words have great insight for us as we consider what trust really looks like:

> In many ways this was a physically tough trip for me. Four of the six members of our group got sick at some point. Jacob and I were covered by severe bug bites, the heat and humidity were intense, not to mention the emotional impact of feeling so small against the vastness of Haiti's need....All of these annoyances forced me to face the fact that I've become accustomed to a life of absolute comfort. If I don't like the heat, I turn on the air. If I'm hungry, I walk to the refrigerator. If I'm sick, I run to Walgreens. If the bugs and critters are thick, I call an exterminator or grab a pair of large shoes. On the

living with less so your family has more   105

whole, Americans have an incredibly low tolerance to anything that makes us the least bit uncomfortable, because at all times we have access to whatever we want to make life a little bit better.

In Haiti I had access to what came in my suitcase. That's it. This forced me to tolerate challenges with little more than faith, determination, and ineffective bug spray. I discovered all ran thin after a couple days.

They say you know the strength of your faith when it's all you have to hang on to. This is probably true, but the problem is we are surrounded by so many vices that few of us ever get to the place where it's all we have left.[8]

Isn't that the truth? We don't really get to experience faith—true faith—until we have nothing else left to cling to. But most of us don't allow ourselves ever to get to that place. "It's too risky," we rationalize. Yep, faith is risky. But never letting God really be God in our lives also is risky—it robs us of the opportunity to watch Him work in ways that only He can.

When God sent an angel to tell Mary that she was going to give birth to Jesus, she was astonished at the message. She knew she'd never slept with a man, so if she were pregnant it would have to be a miracle. But she didn't resist God's unexpected message: "I'm the Lord's maid, ready to serve. Let it be with me just as you say." (Luke 1:28, *The Message*) She trusted her God. If He had other plans for her life, then so be it. Honestly, I (Mark) know that I am not always that quick to trust. I will easily trust God when I can see His activity, but not when He asks me to do something *before* I see Him work. In fact, sometimes I fight God for a while before I

[8] www.michelecushatt.com; Haiti Journal: The Other Side; June 15, 2009; used with permission

finally agree to trust Him. I want to learn to respond to God more like Mary.

After Mary learned she was pregnant, she went to visit her relative Elizabeth, who was also pregnant. Elizabeth's pregnancy was also a miracle because she was way past child-rearing years; it's estimated that Elizabeth was in her nineties. Elizabeth greets Mary and confirms Mary's trust in God when she says, "Blessed woman, who believed what God said, believed every word would come true!" (Luke 1:45, *The Message*) In today's language, Elizabeth would have said, "Girl, because you've trusted you are going to have the ride of a lifetime!"

GRAB A FRONT-ROW SEAT TO WATCH GOD WORK!

Consider the picture of Indiana Jones stepping off the cliff. It's the first step that's the hardest. Stepping out in faith is hard, but if you're going to choose to live with less, you're going to need to know how to walk by faith. One of our favorite stories about faith in the Bible is when Jesus invited Peter to walk on the water. Now talk about a risk—a real and literal step of faith. Let's take a look at this story and see what wisdom we can glean:

> As soon as the meal was finished, [Jesus] insisted that the disciples get in the boat and go on ahead to the other side while he dismissed the people. With the crowd dispersed, he climbed the mountain so he could be by himself and pray. He stayed there alone, late into the night.
>
> Meanwhile, the boat was far out to sea when the wind came up against them and they were battered by the waves. At about four o'clock in the morning, Jesus came toward them walking on the water. They were scared out of their wits. "A ghost!" they said, crying out in terror.

But Jesus was quick to comfort them. "Courage, it's me. Don't be afraid."

Peter, suddenly bold, said, "Master, if it's really you, call me to come to you on the water."

He said, "Come ahead."

Jumping out of the boat, Peter walked on the water to Jesus. But when he looked down at the waves churning beneath his feet, he lost his nerve and started to sink. He cried, "Master, save me!"

Jesus didn't hesitate. He reached down and grabbed his hand. Then he said, "Faint-heart, what got into you?"

The two of them climbed into the boat, and the wind died down. The disciples in the boat, having watched the whole thing, worshiped Jesus, saying, "This is it! You are God's Son for sure!" (Matthew 14:22–32, *The Message*)

What a real life picture of faith! Using this story and an acrostic of the word "faith," let's glean five faith principles for our lives:

Fully obey—Jesus insisted that the disciples get in the boat and head out without Him. They didn't necessarily understand why, but they did as he said. When God asks us to walk by faith, we don't always understand the plan, but we can learn to trust that God does have a plan. We are continuing to learn how His plan is always better than ours. His abundance is beyond our ability to fathom until we experience it.

Accept God's invitation—Peter didn't just jump out of the boat; he had a conversation with the Lord that prompted the invitation to come. Stepping out in faith outside of God's will is foolishness. When we hear God's direction and it is congruent with God's truth and confirmed by believers around us, then we need to get out of the boat. Some of our decisions to live with less will likely require us to accept God's invitation and get out of the boat.

Internalize a childlike faith—I love Peter's childlike faith. He often speaks before he thinks about what he is doing. Many times we rationalize ourselves right out of obedience because we think too hard about the logic of what God is asking. Children are rarely logical in their thinking. And God is rarely logical—His ways are not our ways. Pursuing the less-is-more life may sometimes feel like it defies logic. If you feel that way, you might be living out real faith.

Take the step—Peter got out of the boat but the other eleven disciples stayed in the safety of the boat. They didn't even ask Jesus if they could walk to Him on the water. When we stay in the boat we miss the blessing of experiencing God at work firsthand. When we get out of the boat of our comfort zone and step into the water of faith, we experience blessings that only come when taking steps of faith.

Hold steady—Peter stepped out of the boat and began to walk toward Jesus, but the minute he took his eyes off Jesus and began to look at the waves around him, he began to sink. Too often we look at the mountains instead of the one who can move mountains—and that's when we begin to doubt. We have to keep our eyes on God, trusting His ways. Proverbs 3:5 tells us, "Trust in the Lord with all your heart and lean not on your own understanding." When Peter looked down at the waves he couldn't understand how he was actually walking on the water. Trying to understand from a human perspective caused him to lose faith. We, too, will have the temptation to take our eyes off of Jesus and begin to sink. Choosing to stand up to adult peer pressure requires us to keep eye contact with God.[9]

[9] Adapted from: Jill Savage, *Real Moms…Real Jesus* (Chicago: Moody Publishers, 2009), 198–200

We can't imagine anything more rewarding than watching God do His stuff. In order to do that, however, we have to let go. We have to turn our fear into faith. We have to give God opportunities to work. Living on less gives wonderful opportunities to have a front-row seat to watch God work. We may be just ordinary people, but we have an extraordinary God!

Jesus, this faith thing is so hard, but I know when I depend on myself only, I don't give You an opportunity to work in my life. Help me to learn to hear Your voice more clearly and take the steps of faith You ask me to take. Help me to find the balance between responsibility and the risk-taking that faith requires. More than anything, help me to get to know You more, listen to You better, and trust You in my daily life. In Jesus' name, amen.

let's talk about it

After reading this chapter, I've been thinking about...

I have seen God work in our life when...

I struggle trusting God in these areas of my life...

chapter 9

community: you can't do this alone

WE DESCRIBE OURSELVES AS BEING MARRIED TWENTY-SEVEN YEARS, seventeen of them happily. Our marriage has definitely had its ups and downs. The downs were pretty bad—so bad that we weren't sure we were even going to make it. Our downs have included recurring arguments about money, sex, anger and handling extended family, just to name a few. We've had to relearn how to handle conflict in a healthy manner, find a new understanding of why God created sex, and deal with baggage we both carried in from previous relationships. After getting to the other side of our train wreck of a marriage, we determined that we would share openly and honestly about our relationship challenges. In speaking, writing, preaching and talking with other couples, we share the good, the bad and even the ugly in an effort to let couples know they're not alone.

After hearing our stories, couples will often ask if we've had a hidden camera in their home, because their experiences and challenges are so similar to ours. Others will thank us for our honesty because it gives them hope that maybe they can make it through their own challenging season. Most people just appreciate knowing that they are normal.

The responses we get when we share about real life illustrate the power of community. Community gives you hope, encourages you along the journey, helps cast your vision for the future, and lets you know that you're doing okay. When you hang with other people who understand what your life is like, you're more likely to stay on course. However, when you try to go it alone or hang too often with people who don't share your vision and values, you risk becoming disillusioned. Once discouragement sets in, it's very easy to get "vision drift," when our hearts and minds are more influenced by our culture than by the vision and direction we've determined are best for our family.

If we're going to swim upstream, we'll need to be swimming with other families that are doing the same thing. We need their fresh ideas to keep up with a changing economy. At times we'll need their hope when we hit a tough spot and want to give up. And we'll need their inspiration to stay committed for the long haul. So where do we find these families? How do we make the connections that will keep us on track with our vision? Let's look at five places where we can find regular support for living with less so that our family can have more.

THE NEIGHBORHOOD

The physical community we live in will definitely influence our perspective. If we're living above our means in the midst of other families who are very concerned about the things money can buy, we'll find ourselves feeling isolated and alone in the journey. We've known people who have downsized to a neighborhood where they have a better chance of finding like-minded families—families who are happy with a simpler home and lifestyle. Is this a change that could help you stay on track with the less-is-more vision?

Some friends who live in Minnesota found this to be true for them. Here's their experience and perspective:

We don't live in a palatial house at all, but I couldn't trade it for any other abode around. It's not because of the way it looks, but because of the neighbors that surround it. When we bought this home, we were insistent that we would buy a home that would be welcoming of our one-income budget.

I'm so grateful God provided us with a neighborhood full of average homes where a lot of the wives are stay-at-home moms too. There aren't fences up around the yards. The kids spend summers and hours after school playing baseball in the cul-de-sac and kickball in the backyard. On Sunday evenings in the summer we all gather around a fire pit in our neighbors' backyard and chat about the week ahead. We also have a Tuesday Bible study that's been meeting for eighteen years!

It truly is a community that encourages me in the simple lifestyle we must have in order for me to stay home. We share a lot of the same values, and I'm so glad that I'm not forced to earn more money so that we can have pristine yards, shiny new vehicles, and kids with the latest electronics. It's important to consider these things when you purchase a home. Your neighbors will be an influence on you and your family—make sure that it's a positive environment for your family values.

Like our friends have found, getting to know the neighbors is a helpful tool in finding families who live nearby who share similar vision and values. If you didn't grow up in a family that "neighbored," you might not know where to start. A good place to begin is with food. If you want to start small, choose one night a week to invite a neighborhood family over for dessert. Enjoy an hour or so of getting to know one another, sharing stories, and letting the kids play. If you enjoy the evening, pursue more time together. If not, be content waving and saying hello when you carry out the garbage.

If you're not intimated by hospitality, then hosting a neighborhood summer picnic can be a great way to get to know a wider circle of people who live close by. Ask everyone to bring lawn chairs as well as meat to grill and a dish to pass. One mom hosted a neighborhood Easter-egg hunt, which allowed their family to connect with families they hadn't met before. She reported that she got to know some new neighbors and everyone had a wonderful time!

CHURCH

A church community is a great way to find like-minded families with similar goals and vision. Depending on the size and style of the church, you'll likely find the congregation to be very diverse economically, so it may take a little bit of effort to find families that really share the same vision you have.

The above strategies we shared for getting to know families in your neighborhood work well with your church family too. If your church's Sunday-school classes are organized by season of life (young marrieds, parents, parents of teenagers, etc.), that may assist in your search to find like-minded families.

If your church offers small groups, joining one or organizing your own group could be very helpful in creating a community of families with similar goals and lifestyles. If your church requires small-group training, take the initiative and complete the training. Then invite families to join that you feel would match yours well. Living with less requires a community approach, and a strong small group can help. In our small group, we've seen this happen over and over. Recently, when we put in our garden, one of the guys in our small group offered to let us borrow his tiller so we didn't have to purchase or rent one. Then he even came over and tilled the yard himself! The guys enjoyed working together, and we got a new garden out of it. There's no need for each of us to own the same equipment—we can share and help one another out. This same friend needed a place to store some woodworking equipment he no longer had room for in his garage. We offered him a place to store it in our machine shed—living in the country, we have extra outbuildings including a barn and machine shed that we make available to our friends. He told Mark that he is welcome to use the woodworking equipment anytime. Having a great community around you can actually help you live with less.

Small-group relationships can also strengthen your spiritual foundation while you are working to live out your priorities. When one of our small-group members wanted to change jobs so that she would have a less stressful office environment and fewer work hours, we began praying for her and her desire to "downsize" her job. When she wavers on her resolve to make the change to better match her priorities, we provide the encouragement and accountability to keep her focused on her vision.

SUPPORT GROUPS

Jill's moms group was her life preserver in our early years of living on one income. Being with other moms who were also living with less kept her from drowning in circumstances that often felt so overwhelming. A good moms group can provide childcare trades, coupon exchanges and clothing swaps, as well as speakers and discussions about living with less and parenting with purpose.

If you have preschoolers, the best place to locate a moms group near you is online at www.mops.org. MOPS, which stands for Mothers of Preschoolers, has moms groups all over the world. Simply enter your ZIP code on the Web site and they'll let you know where you can find the closest group to your home. If you're past the preschool years or don't have a MOPS group close to you, consider starting your own. The Hearts at Home book *Creating the Moms Group You've Been Looking For* has step-by-step instructions on how to start your own moms group.

Dads need support, too, but in our community the concept of a "dads group" has yet to take off. Still, Mark has found support in church small groups and friendships with other frugal dads. Spending time with other dads who have similar values provides much-needed support and encouragement.

ONLINE

In today's world, anyone with a computer can connect to a like-minded community with the simple click of a mouse. It doesn't get much easier than that. Do a search on phrases like "frugal families," "frugal living," "simple living," "one income" and "money-saving tips," and you'll find more than enough encouragement to keep you going. We've included some of our favorites in the appendix at the back of this book.

If you've not explored the blog world, you'll find plenty of encouragement there as well. A Google search for some of the above words (www.blogsearch.google.com) will likely score you an array of blogs to read through. Once you find some blogs you like, you can have the posts delivered right to you if you subscribe to the blog via RSS Feed or an e-mail subscription! This connects you to an always-available online community that understands what your life is like. Because we don't live in a typical neighborhood, we've found the online community to be invaluable in keeping us connected to other families who are intentionally investing in family relationships.

Other online resources include chat rooms, forums and bulletin boards that discuss living with less. The bulletin board is one of the most active parts of the Hearts at Home Web site (www.hearts-at-home.org). This is where moms connect with other moms who are keeping their families their first priority and their hearts at home.

BOOKS

A family that is serious about living with less has to keep consuming a steady diet of books that encourage you to live differently. We both try to read at least one book a year that encourages us to live with less and give our family more. Two of our favorites, which we have read more than once, are *Margin* by Dr. Richard Swenson and *Making Room for Life* by Randy Frazee. Another highly recommended resource is *Freedom of Simplicity* by Richard Foster. In fact, the book you are holding might be an annual read for you or a great gift to a family member or friend who could use this type of encouragement.

If it's been a while since you've been to the public library, take an hour or so to explore and see what continuing education resources you can find to keep you encouraged in the direction you're setting for your family. Many communities have a coffee-shop bookstore where you can easily spend a couple of hours. Sometimes we'll have a date night and explore one of these larger bookstores, where you can select a book, find a chair and start reading. If you and your spouse head into the evening with the goal of finding some great books that help you live with less, budget more effectively and increase family time, you can read aloud to each other over a cup of coffee. A date night like this can be packed with encouragement that will build you up and equip you to give your family more while living with less.

Lord, when You lived on this earth You showed us that we are not designed to live life alone. You lived in community with the disciples and others who were close to You. Help me to value the relationships and resources around me. Give me the vision to pursue community when it feels easier to just take care of myself and my family. Help me to be a lifelong learner who seeks out encouragement to keep my vision strong and my strategies fresh. In Jesus' name, amen.

let's talk about it

After reading about community, I've been thinking about ...

In our current situation, we have these obstacles to pursuing community ...

One place I'd like for us to be more intentional about pursuing community is ...

part 3: actions

WE STARTED WITH VISION. Then we explored the attitudes needed to stay committed to the vision. Now we're going to explore the practical actions that help us to live out our vision strategically.

Over the next nine chapters we're going to encourage you to think proactively about your financial decisions. Combined with the right attitudes, these proven strategies can help you make more from less. Right attitudes coupled with wise actions will allow a family to live successfully with less.

Because this section is about taking action on our plans, each of these chapters will be arranged around the acronym PLAN: P-Prepare, L-Listen, A-Adjust and N-Navigate. These sections will lay out proactive plans and strategies for living with less money. Many of the suggested strategies have been compiled from "living with less" discussions on Jill's blog over the past year.

Every person is unique. Every family is unique. There's no single right way to make "less is more" happen in your family. This section is designed to help us think about areas of our lives that we often put on autopilot. The river of life moves along and we get caught in the current without even realizing it. This section will help us evaluate that current and determine if we need to take a different route to our destination.

Are you catching the vision? Evaluating your attitudes? Ready to make some real changes that can help you redefine your priorities? Turn the page and explore the actions that can bring your vision to life!

chapter 10

finances: budget is not a bad word and cash really is in vogue

WITHIN WEEKS OF THEIR WEDDING, our daughter and son-in-law participated in Dave Ramsey's *Financial Peace* video course on finances. What a wonderful financial foundation they set for their newly established marriage. If we had taken a similar course when we were first married, we would likely have saved ourselves many mistakes over the years. We simply didn't know much about managing money, and much of what we know now came from twenty-seven years of enrollment in the school of hard knocks. For much of that time, we took on debt, saved little and lived pretty much from paycheck to paycheck.

Last year we participated in the same course through our church. We found ourselves both affirmed and challenged. We felt reassured in some of the wise financial decisions we had made over the years, especially with regard to our commitment to pay off debt. We felt challenged to get even more control of our spending, budgeting and saving. We determined that we had to increase our communication about financial issues and better share the financial responsibilities of balancing the checkbook, creating a monthly spending plan, and saving proactively.

Finances can be a major source of conflict in marriage. We've certainly had our share of quarrels about money over the years. What we have learned, however, is that conflict is more likely to happen when we react to life rather than plan for it. When we're dealing with finances reactively, conflict increases. When we're dealing with finances proactively, conflict decreases. With that in mind, let's look at some ways that we can be proactive in managing our money.

PREPARE

Most of us underestimate the time needed to manage the family finances. It's really not about big blocks of time, but rather daily, smaller pieces. If you haven't really worked together on finances, however, you'll probably need a little bit of extra time to prepare a plan.

If you've never established any type of spending plan, you may want to start by looking at every purchase you make over a month's time. Some couples choose to do this by carrying a notebook and pen and recording every purchase they make during a chosen month. Others use a computer program such as Quicken, which allows you to attach a category name to every purchase you make by check, credit card or debit card. With the push of a button, a report of how much you have spent in a category is at your fingertips. It's not important how you track your spending habits; it's simply important that you track them somehow. This isn't something you have to do every month. Just do it once a year to establish a new spending plan or evaluate the one you are using.

It's our job to manage our money well, and preparing a spending plan is how we do that best. If we don't manage our money, our money will manage us. Unfortunately, that's how many of us end up in debt and scraping to make ends meet. Once we have a picture of our spending habits, we can create a template for a spending plan. The goal is to put a label on every dollar of our income. This assures us that we are managing what comes in and determining how it is saved or spent. If you need sample forms for creating your spending plan, you can find a wide array of free financial tools online at www.crown.org/tools. (In addition to their online resources, Crown Ministries also offers wonderful money management courses you can find at many local churches.)

Once you've established your plan, you'll need to revisit it each month to make sure it allows adequately for upcoming expenses. For instance, when we know that we'll soon be taking a trip to visit extended family who live several hours away, we have to adjust the fuel budget for that month. We'll likely need two extra tanks of gas that month in order to get to our destination and back home again. If an extra $80 is going to gas, then we have to adjust another category to accommodate the changed expense.

When creating a spending plan, don't forget to prepare for the unexpected. We never "expect" the car to break down, but every car does at some time or another. We never "expect" for the kids to need new shoes, but there's no way to stop their feet from growing. We never "expect" for our water heater to go out, but most don't last longer than fifteen years. Make sure you are setting aside money for emergencies and unexpected but unavoidable expenses. Families that don't plan for the unexpected invariably reach for the credit card to handle them. We know this from experience, because that's how we handled these so-called emergencies for many years. We've learned our lesson, though, because it took a long time and a lot more money to pay it back with interest. A lack of planning doesn't constitute an emergency. But this leads us to another financial plan we might need.

Set up a regular time to meet about your spending plan. We've found that Monday evenings, after the kids are in bed, work well for us. (It usually takes us about thirty to sixty minutes.) If you're not already in the habit of doing this, what time during the week might work for you?

If you are carrying any debt beyond a mortgage and a car loan, you'll want to set a plan in motion for debt reduction. Debt can strangle families and their dreams to really live on less. The Bible says "the borrower is servant to the lender." (Proverbs 22:7) When our money is tied up in paying debt, it can't be used for your family's needs or God's work.

If debt is a part of your life, it's not the end of the world. But you need to draw a line in the sand and determine that it *is* the beginning of the end of living with debt. Creating—and implementing—an aggressive plan for paying down debt is essential. Dave Ramsey calls it the "Debt Snowball." Crown Ministries labels it "Accelerated Debt Payoff." It doesn't matter what you call it; it just matters that you do it! The premise of these plans is that you list out your debts, paying off the smallest balance first. Once the first debt is paid off, the monthly payment you were making on that debt can be applied to the second debt. This is what "accelerates" or "snowballs" the debt reduction. Without a plan, we'd likely make just the minimum monthly payment on each debt. Lenders keep those payment amounts low to keep us in debt longer so they can collect as much interest as possible. While they want us to believe that they are dedicated to keeping our payments "affordable," what they are really dedicated to is filling their pockets with the interest they glean from our overspending and underplanning. List your debts and set a plan in motion to aggressively pay them off. You can find a free resource online to help with this at www.whatsthecost.com (click on "snowballing").

Another tip we found helpful with debt elimination is to call your credit-card providers and ask them to lower your interest rates. If you've always paid at least the minimum balance on time, they will often say yes.

A well-balanced plan will help you manage your money instead of dealing with the repercussions of letting your money manage you. Tracking spending, planning how you will spend every dollar, and paying off debt are important preparation for properly managing the money God has given us.

LISTEN

Communication is an important part of any successful partnership. A commitment to live on less will test even the most solid marriage because you are choosing what you feel is best for your family, not necessarily something that is easy to do. Living differently than the world requires you to link hearts to share the vision and link arms to make the vision a reality.

You'll want to begin with a fresh start. Don't play the blame game. Don't bring up past mistakes or point fingers at your spouse. Decide you will work together and go at it with full force. Commit together to the realities of the new spending habits that you decide are needed.

While forging a "less is more" life with another person, you'll inevitably end up frustrated with one another. Your personalities and temperaments will clash somewhere along the way. Despite what drew you together in the first place, most married couples find that they really are wonderfully incompatible and even perfect paradoxes. He's a night owl, but she's a morning bird. He loves spicy foods, while she prefers mild. He's an introvert, and she's an extrovert. He's a spender, but she's a saver.

When it comes to money, you're likely opposites in some way, just as we are! Jill is the planner, the organizer, and the one who is always serious about money. Mark, on the other hand, has way too much fun in life to deal with money. In Dave Ramsey's words, Jill is a "nerd," and Mark is a "free spirit." Nerds set the plan and stick to the plan. Free spirits have no use for a plan. But we do complement one another. Jill needs to loosen up some of the time, and Mark needs to tighten up on occasion. By valuing our differences, we can actually strengthen our partnership and fortify our resolve.

Listen to what your partner is saying during the planning process—not just the words, but the heart of what he's trying to get across. Don't discount his perceptions, thoughts or concerns simply because they are different from yours. What is he truly communicating? What are the fears behind the words? Don't get snagged by how something is said; instead, listen for the heart of what he is trying to say. Practice "reflective listening." This is when you reflect back to your spouse what you've heard him say before you respond to what has been communicated. For instance:

Mark: It feels like I never have any money to spend. I have to go to Mom to ask for money.

Jill: What I hear you saying is that you feel that your hands are tied when it comes to finances and you feel that I'm more in charge of money than you are. Would that be correct?

Mark: Yes, that would be correct.

That interaction hasn't solved the problem at hand—yet—but it has done something very important. It has assured the frustrated person that he has been heard, which is a prerequisite for making progress together toward your goal.

Once someone feels heard, the need to continue the argument diminishes. Once the ire is removed from the interaction, communication can more easily occur. If we were to continue the above conversation, Jill might move into questioning mode. "Can you help me understand what situations have caused you to feel this way?" or "Help me understand what we could change so you would feel more of a partner in our finances." These nondefensive statements or questions invite conversation and resolve. Listening to each other is an important part of the PLAN of finances.

ADJUST

Once you've prepared your spending plan and you're allowing your spending decisions to guide you, you'll likely have to make some adjustments. First off, you may have to adjust your attitude. If you're not used to thinking about a spending plan, you might feel resentment about what you perceive to be limits on your fun. This is a common feeling, but it usually results from shortsightedness. The plan is in place so that you can live out your larger vision. The goal is less spending, which leads to less stress, so that you will have the time and energy you need to invest in your family relationships.

"But living with less money is stressful to me!" you might respond. And for many people it is. That's why we introduced the attitudes before the actions. Without a right perspective, a right heart, a right attitude, the actions can be very frustrating. Adjust your perspective to the big picture and you'll find yourself more committed and less frustrated.

NAVIGATE

Everyone has to make personal decisions about how to live out the financial plan that is decided on. However, we've found some specific strategies that have helped us navigate the living-with-less money maze. Maybe some of these will help you plot your own course.

calendar

Decide what night of the week you will commit to talk about money each week. Write it on the calendar and protect it. You need that time to work together and strengthen your habits.

use cash

We've found that using cash helps us stick to our spending plan better than anything else. Cash is finite. You either have it or you don't. When we use credit cards, debit cards or checks, we can too easily overspend.

use an envelope system for your cash

By putting the amount of money we allocated in our spending plan for things like food, gas, entertainment, clothes, etc., in separate envelopes, we're aware of how much we have for each category. Some people write their purchases on the outside of the envelopes to keep an eye on what they are spending their money on.

use online bill pay for tithing, recurring payments, transfers to savings, and more

When we switched over to online bill payments, we cut our money management time in half! A few extra minutes of setup time is well worth the relief you'll have knowing your bills will be paid with hardly any work on your part.

For recurring payments that are the same amount each month, your payment automatically goes out on the date you set. If the payment amount is different each month, you'll need to go in and change the amount after you receive each invoice. It's simpler and faster than writing a check, addressing an envelope, and putting the payment in the mailbox.

We also love how automatic payments allow us to be more consistent with our tithing and saving. We have a recurring payment set up for our tithe based upon 10 percent of our income. Two days after each payday, we have an automatic payment set up to send a check to our church. We also have set amounts that automatically transfer from our checking account to our savings account. This assures us that money will be set aside for our emergency fund, future purchases and medical expenses.

divide money management responsibilities

Because of Mark's free-spirited mentality, he was content to let Jill handle all of our finances for many years. This, however, caused resentment in both of us. Mark resented Jill "controlling" the money. Jill resented having to carry all of the responsibilities of our finances. Now we've compromised; Mark reconciles the checkbook every month, and Jill handles bills as well as getting our cash into the appropriate envelopes. At our Monday evening financial meetings, we evaluate the spending plan and make sure our check register is up to date. Now we both understand the bigger financial picture and contribute to managing the money in our family.

recalculate your spending plan at least once a year

As your kids get older or you add another child to the family, expenses change. If you are paying off debts, money needs to be redistributed as you eliminate debts. Life changes and your spending plan will need to flex with those changes.

This may be the first time you've actually worked together to accomplish a single vision for something bigger than a do-it-yourself weekend project. If it is, you'll have some bumps along the way as you learn how to work together more intentionally. Don't be discouraged. In fact, be encouraged! You're making progress in redefining your priorities and living out your vision for your family.

Lord, help us to be proactive about managing our money. We know that You have trusted us with our money and You want us to be good stewards of what You have given us. We need Your help with communication, too. Show us how to listen well and resist defensiveness in our conflicts and conversations. Give us one heart and one mind as we pursue our less-is-more vision. In Jesus' name, amen.

let's talk about it

Since reading this chapter, I've been thinking about...

I am willing to take this step in tracking or planning our finances...

I am willing to make this specific time work weekly to communicate about our finances...

chapter 11

savings, investments and insurance: it's all about the risk

BENJAMIN FRANKLIN ONCE SAID, "A PENNY SAVED IS A PENNY EARNED." That wisdom transcends the ages, and helps us to understand why a savings plan is just as important as a spending plan. Savings has been an area of growth for us. We both wish we had saved more intentionally early on. Doing so would likely have kept us out of debt, made our living-with-less commitment much easier, and prepared us more effectively for retirement. Plus, the whole compound interest thing does so much better over a long period of time. (We'll talk about that more in a few pages.)

Every family needs a savings plan. If you've already got one established, good for you! If you haven't been saving, you can't afford not to. Let's look at a PLAN for savings.

PREPARE

When it comes to saving, there are many different categories to consider. There are short-term savings for purchases, saving for expected but not regular expenses, emergency savings, and saving for the future, which includes insurance and retirement. The difference between a financially prepared family and a financially unprepared family is usually determined by their savings plan. Let's take a closer look at each category of savings.

save for purchases

The world screams all kinds of messages that are supposed to "help" us get what we want: Ninety Days Same as Cash! No Interest for 12 Months! No Payments for 18 Months! In reality, those plans won't help us. They'll help the retailer who is betting on the fact that we won't pay our bill in the established amount of time, so they'll be able to make lots of money on interest.

Instead, we need to save up for our purchases, and whenever possible, pay cash. It may sound old-fashioned, but it's one of the best ways to purchase anything. Here are some purchases we need to be saving for:

- Furniture replacement
- Car replacement
- Clothing
- Home improvement
- Gifts (birthday, graduation and Christmas)

Many people find it helpful to open separate accounts for each of these categories. This strategy allows you to see your balance at a glance. It also keeps the temptation to "borrow" from one account to boost another at bay.

save for the "unexpected expected"

Yes, you read that right. We need to save for things that seem always to catch us off guard, but that we really should expect. These are the living expenses that will present themselves at some point in time, but aren't necessarily regular monthly expenses. These are the "unexpected expected" we need to save for—and note that not everyone will have expenses in these categories:

- Homeowner's or renter's insurance (if you pay an annual or semiannual premium)
- Health insurance (if you pay an annual or semiannual premium that does not automatically come out of your paycheck)
- Health expenses (prescriptions, co-pays, etc.)
- Auto insurance (if you pay an annual or semiannual premium)
- Deductibles (auto, health, home insurance deductibles)
- Vehicle registration and/or license plates/stickers
- Self-employment taxes
- Property taxes (if you don't escrow them with your mortgage lender)
- Household repairs
- Car repairs
- Vacation
- Summer camp/lessons for kids

Because these types of expenses happen anywhere from every other month to once a year, we have to annualize the estimated or known amount and divide it by twelve to determine the amount we need to save monthly. This preparation process is essential to keeping a handle on all the household expenses. If these types of expenses aren't accommodated in the monthly budget, the unprepared family will turn to credit cards.

save for emergencies

Money experts suggest having up to six months of living expenses in a savings account. For many of us, up until the recent economic crisis, this seemed like a nice but unnecessary idea. Now, with so many companies downsizing or closing their doors, we're seeing the importance of this kind of savings. Our unstable economy has illustrated the need for a stable emergency fund even more.

If you have no emergency savings, just start with something, however small it may be. Make sure you are depositing a regular amount in an emergency savings fund from each paycheck until you have a full six months of living expenses socked away.

There are lots of easy and creative ways to save money. Here are some of the best suggestions we've heard:

- Put loose change and dollar bills into a jar. Once a month, deposit the contents into your savings account.
- After you have paid off a debt, keep paying that same amount—into your savings. (If you're doing the debt snowball, this would happen after you pay off your last debt!)
- Move a month's worth of savings into a one-month certificate of deposit (CD). When that matures, roll the principal and interest into another one-month CD. Eventually, you'll have enough profit to reinvest in a higher interest-paying CD.
- Give up something you "always" have to have—cigarettes, bottled water, coffee drinks, candy—and save this money in a jar instead.
- Next time you get a raise or bonus, put it in the bank rather than expanding your budget.
- If you pay off something like a car, start saving toward your next car with the money you were previously paying each month. You may be able to actually pay cash for your next car. Imagine: You'd have no car payment and save thousands of dollars in interest!

save for the future

The wise family thinks about saving for retirement and the future. This is hard for us to think about while raising a family, because it feels so far away and so irrelevant to our immediate concerns.

However, it's very important that we prepare and plan for the truly unexpected as well as for retirement—and the earlier, the better.

This is where compound interest can work for us. Compound interest is, very simply, the effect of interest being paid on interest. The principal—the original amount deposited in an interest-bearing account—earns interest. Then the interest is added to the principal, and that new amount now earns more interest. The cycle continues, and over a long period of time, our money will multiply.

When thinking about the future, we need to include both insurance and investments. Insurance includes life insurance, disability insurance, property insurance and health insurance. Investments include mutual funds, money-market funds and more. Too many of us tend to skimp on insurance when money is tight. But this is not a place to skimp at all. In fact, families who choose to live with less especially need to make sure they are prepared for disasters (insurance) and for the future (investments). We will discuss these in more detail in the "navigate" part of this chapter.

LISTEN

When it comes to money, every one of us has a filter that we bring into marriage. This filter is based upon our experience with money growing up, our experience (or inexperience) managing our own money, and our perceptions and misperceptions about money. Because of this, we have to find common ground and a shared strategy for how we will manage our money together. Even after twenty-six years of marriage, we find that our default filters can sneak into our conversations. That's why each of us has to listen to our spouse's fears, concerns and frustrations. We need to reassure each other that we are committed to working together to move away from the patterns of the past and make our present and future what we long for it to be.

Two minds are better than one. Think through and discuss every area of life that you need to save for. Discuss realistic monthly saving amounts based upon your income. Listen to your spouse's suggestions. Determine together the best way to proceed in your savings plan.

ADJUST

One of the hardest things about saving is that you have to exchange short-term comfort for long-term stability. That's a hard adjustment for some of us to make. We want to live in the moment more than we want to live in the future. Adjusting our perspective to value both short-term and long-term needs helps us to successfully create a savings plan.

Another adjustment you'll need to make is to move from appreciating instant gratification to accepting delayed gratification. The concept of "12 months same as cash," is widely accepted as a good way to make large purchases. *Need a new computer? Hey, we've got the perfect plan for you! A new camcorder? Don't worry—you won't owe a thing until next summer!* These kinds of programs are so tempting, given our instant-gratification mindset. But using them can be playing with financial fire.

In a 12-months-same-as-cash program, if you are one day late on a payment, or if there is any balance on the account after twelve months, you'll be required to pay all of the interest from the date of purchase on the full price of the loan. It doesn't matter that you've paid most of it off. It doesn't matter that you were on time for every other payment. One wrong move and you will pay for it big time. This is how companies make their money!

You can, however, do your own version of this program... in your savings account! Saving up requires you to wait a little while longer for your purchase, but it is often a much better strategy. Once you've saved the amount of money needed to make your purchase, you withdraw the money and buy the item *with cash*. Now you own your new piece of furniture, or your new video camera, or your new-to-you-but-really-used motorcycle that you've always wanted. When we adjust from instant gratification to delayed gratification, we become much better money managers. And staying out of debt is an extremely important strategy to live with less successfully.

NAVIGATE
savings

We'll be more likely to succeed if we can automate saving. If your employer allows you to divide your paycheck up and deposit it into multiple accounts, take advantage of that benefit. If you're working with a financial planner on retirement, ask the planner about options for taking monthly payments directly out of your paycheck or your checking account. It's so much easier to save when you don't see the money you are putting away.

Because we don't have the option to divide up our paychecks, we have set up an automatic account transfer with our bank for our short-term savings. We add up our predetermined amounts for each category and make one transfer each month from our checking to our savings. For simplicity, we keep just one savings account, but we have different categories we're saving toward within that account, so we have developed a simple bookkeeping strategy. In a three-ring binder, we keep a separate handwritten balance sheet for each category so we know how much we have set aside for Christmas, property taxes, car repairs, etc. Each month we update the balance when the account transfer is made. If any money is withdrawn or transferred from savings to checking to cover a purchase in that category, we update the balance sheet at the time of purchase. Our friend Beth has about seven savings accounts at an online bank—one each for her emergency fund, travel, Christmas, kitchen renovation, etc. She has repeating transfers set up to automatically move money into each account each month. She says it's a great way to save money and once it's set up you don't ever have to think about it.

While we haven't opened a savings account with an online bank, our married children have informed us that the best interest rates are found with online banks, not with brick-and-mortar banks in your neighborhood. As long as your account is with an FDIC member bank, it doesn't matter whether the bank is online or in your neighborhood—what's most important is that you are putting money in a bank somewhere.

Some financial experts, including Dave Ramsey, suggest putting savings that you need access to into a money-market account. While earning some interest, this allows you easy access to the money with no penalty for withdrawal.[10] It's important to note that usually these types of accounts restrict the number of withdrawals each month, so you want to use this type of account for funds that you need only occasional access to.

insurance—transferring risk

While insurance isn't technically savings, it is thinking toward the future, so we've included it in our discussion in this chapter. A less-is-more family needs to have insurance coverage for what they hope won't happen. Disability insurance and life insurance are extremely important. Disability insurance ensures that you will continue to receive a regular salary if a wage earner in the family is disabled and unable to work. Life insurance provides income for your family in the case of death. And if your "less" includes one

[10] Dave Ramsey, *Financial Peace University Workbook* (Brentwood, Tennessee: The Lampo Group, 2007), 18.

spouse at home, make sure to have enough insurance to cover the economic needs your family would have in the event of a death or disability. You'd be surprised at the economic benefit that spouse brings to your family, despite the lack of income. You don't want it to happen, but you should understand it enough to prepare for the possibility of it.

In thinking about life insurance, the question to ask is, "Who is dependent on what I do?" If others are dependent on you, you need insurance. Many financial experts recommend term life insurance over "whole life." It's much less expensive. Whole life is a forced savings plan that you don't need if you've got a solid savings plan in place. Term life insurance allows you to buy life insurance while you have children and a spouse who are depending on your income. It is good for a term of, say, twenty years, until you no longer have so many people depending on your income. If you are wise about saving and investing, when your term is over, you will no longer need life insurance because your investments and savings will essentially make you self-insured. For example, Gary, a former insurance agent purchased a whole-life policy in 1989 with a $58,000 death benefit from himself. He put in $50 a month for nineteen years, for a total of around $11,400. He says, "When I wised up and replaced my whole-life (investment) insurance with straight term insurance, I cashed [out the whole-life policy]. The cash value was around $12,000—a net return of squat! Now I have $75,0000 of death benefit for $70 a month, and invest $500 a month into a Roth IRA."[11]

Besides disability and life insurance, we obviously need homeowner's or renter's insurance as well as auto insurance. Insurance transfers risk. We don't want to think of the possibility of a fire, a tornado, a burglary or a disaster, but there is no assurance that such

[11] www.daveramsey.com/article/the-truth-about-life-insurance/lifeandmoney_insurance

things won't happen to us. We need insurance to protect our property and our possessions because they add up to a significant amount of money. If we don't have insurance and disaster strikes, we will have no way to cover the costs of replacing our property and/or possessions. One of the biggest mistakes people make with insurance is not evaluating coverage and rates once a year. We have to make sure we are not overinsuring or underinsuring anything. We also have to make sure we're getting the best coverage for our money. If your insurance rates increase, don't hesitate to shop around.

Finally, you need health insurance. Some form of health insurance is necessary for your family. If you have the ability to choose your plan and you've been disciplined about savings, a health insurance plan with a higher deductible will save you money if you're paying all or some of your premium. One family we know made an employment decision based upon how much each company chipped in for health insurance. The father had two companies offering him a position with similar pay, and the decision came down to insurance coverage. Another family we know has chosen an alternative insurance-like organization rather than traditional health insurance. Samaritan Ministries International is a Christian health-care sharing ministry (www.samaritanministries.org). A health-care sharing ministry is made up of loving Christians from around the world who join together to help one another with health-care expenses. While we've never used a health-care sharing ministry in lieu of health insurance and can't vouch for them personally, our friend Brian says that his family's experience has been good in the more than ten years they've participated. Other families have found these strategies helpful for saving on medical expenses:

- Ask your doctor for medication samples when he prescribes medicine for you or a family member. They often have some on hand, and this can mean you spend less at the pharmacy.

- Be proactive about your health and your family's health. Exercise and stay at a healthy weight. This can help you have fewer medical expenses in general.
- Dental care can be less expensive at a dental school (check out www.ada.org). You can help a student learn and save money at the same time.
- Ask for generic prescriptions. Generic medications are much less expensive and no less effective than name-brand medications.
- Familiarize yourself with prescription programs in your community. For example, Meijer offers some antibiotics at no cost to the customer. Cub Foods offers a similar program of $4 antibiotics. If you do a little research in your community you might be surprised to find new ways to save money on medications.
- When the doctor asks for a follow-up visit, ask if you can do it by phone to save the cost of a second co-pay.

investments—money for the future

When Jill thinks about long-term savings, she remembers one of the elderly ladies she cared for in the retirement home where she worked as a teenager. Whenever she had to make a decision, Mrs. Greenwood would advise her, "Don't put all your eggs in one basket, Jill." Whether she was looking for a job or considering what college she'd go to, Mrs. Greenwood's words of wisdom would ring in her ears.

It's wisdom that she's remembered even into her adult years as we have planned for retirement. Diversifying investments is important for wise financial planning. Diversification means to "spread around." This lowers your general risk but sets you up for long-term solid retirement investments.

For retirement planning, we highly suggest a twofold plan. First, take some sort of financial class or read a financial book together. We suggest anything by Crown Ministries, Ellie Kay, Dave Ramsey and Mary Hunt. This will give you a basic understanding of financial terms and financial health. Once you have a basic understanding of financial planning, set up a meeting with a financial planner, who can help you develop a diversified investment plan that will work for you and your family. It's hard to think about retirement when it is so far in the future. But retirement funding is based upon compound interest and as we learned earlier, compound interest works best over a long period of time. A well-balanced (diversified) plan includes a mix of higher-risk investments and lower-risk options—you may consider stocks, bonds, CDs, mutual funds and cash. This is where a financial planner comes into the picture. A good financial planner will give you advice and teach you about investments, but you retain the responsibility for all decisions. This is a great way for husbands and wives to partner together in financial planning.

Savings, insurance and investments are all essential components of being financially responsible. The ability to live with less money can be greatly affected by how we manage each of these "plans" for the future. It is wise money-management to evaluate our savings, discuss the future with our spouse, and commit to the vision of the value of saving.

Lord, we have so much. Sometimes it doesn't feel like it, but compared to the rest of the world, we have so much. Help us to be wise stewards of what You have trusted us with. Give us the self-control needed to move from instant gratification to delayed gratification. Help us to make wise decisions about insurance. And show us how to save for purchases, save for the unexpected, and save for our future.
In Jesus' name, amen.

———————*let's talk about it*———————

While reading this chapter I realized...

When it comes to saving for purchases, I'd like to see us save toward...

In thinking about insurance, some steps I'd like for us to take are...

When it comes to investments, I'd like for us to...

chapter 12

food and clothing: have your cake and eat it too

FOOD IS A NEED, NOT A WANT. It is the fuel our bodies must have. It's foundational to physical health. From a financial perspective, however, food can either make or break our family's budget. We've come to realize that grocery purchases are the line item in our spending plan that we are able to control the most. With some time and effort, we can actually learn to buy more with less money.

On the average grocery run, we'll likely purchase food as well as health and beauty supplies. If you shop at a megastore like Super-Target or Super Walmart, you probably add in household items as well as basic clothing needs. Shopping is shopping, so the strategies used in one kind of store typically apply to other kinds of stores. Therefore, we'll use this chapter to discuss a general purchasing PLAN for those everyday items our families need.

PREPARE

Jill hates to shop. We know. It's quite rare to find a woman who doesn't like to shop. But we also know she's not alone. The more she shares that she doesn't like to shop, the more she finds other women who dislike it too. Regardless of whether you consider shopping a necessary evil or one of your favorite pastimes, we can all agree that it has to get done.

Going to the grocery store takes a good amount of time. But did you know that getting ready to go to the grocery store is one of the most important steps we can take to save money? You're likely to purchase more when you shop without a list than when you shop with a plan in mind, so let's look at five steps of preparation that allow us to buy more at the grocery store with less money:

1. Pantry Scan. When we make meals from food we already own, we save our family a lot of money. Take an inventory of what food you have in the pantry, the refrigerator and the freezer. Take note of items you already have on hand to plan for meals. (Once my kids were able to spell and write, I asked them to help with this preparation step. I do the looking, call out the items we have on hand, and they write it down. We only do major shopping once a month so while this takes some time, it's an important part of spending less at the store.) Don't forget to check if you need household products like toilet paper, paper towels and laundry detergent and health and beauty supplies such as shampoo, Band-Aids, toothpaste and soap.

2. Meal Plan. Once we know what ingredients and food items we have on hand, I am able to sit down with the calendar and plan out our meals for a period of time. Because I hate to shop, I usually plan out four weeks of meals. (While I make one large shopping trip a month, I usually make one or two smaller trips to buy perishables including milk, fresh fruit and vegetables.) Other people I know do one or two weeks of meals at a time. Looking at the calendar lets me plan around our family's schedule of ball games, church meetings, etc. On a busy evening I can plan a Crock-Pot meal, and on a less busy day, I can plan a meal that takes a bit more preparation. Don't forget leftovers when planning meals. I try to put "Savage Buffet" on the meal plan once a week to ensure that we use all the leftovers in our refrigerator. Once your meal plan is completed, think through all the ingredients you will need for the meals. If they're not in the pantry, note them for the shopping list you'll create in the next step.

3. Shopping List. When we run out of something, we note it on a continuous shopping list kept on the side of the refrigerator. With the continuous shopping list, inventory and meal plan in hand, we can begin to create the list we'll use at the grocery store.

Several years ago, we created a grocery list on our computer. This list includes all of the items we regularly purchase for our family in the order they're found in the grocery store. If we need an item, we check the box next to the item. If we know we already have something, we cross it off the list. This keeps us from questioning ourselves later when we come across an item that hasn't been marked in some way. Whether you use a prepared computer list or you create a handwritten list every time you shop, just make sure you create a list to guide your purchasing decisions.

4. Coupons. Most of us either love them or hate them. There are entire books and Web sites dedicated to helping you save money with coupons. We're not die-hard coupon fanatics, but we do find they save us money. By clipping them and storing them according to the expiration date, we're able to quickly clean out our coupon envelope once a month. Once the shopping list is made, we look through our coupons to see if we have any for the things on our shopping list. If a coupon is found, I mark the item on the list and note any purchasing requirements on the list (e.g., save $1 when you buy two). We then paper-clip the coupons to the list to make it much easier at checkout.

5. Price-matching. Most major grocery stores will match the prices of other grocery store sales if you bring in an ad for proof. We keep our grocery-store ads in a file folder and update them each week. A quick glance through the ads helps us to secure the best prices of all the stores in our town while shopping at only one. Again, we make a note on our shopping list of any items we want to alert the checkout person to price-match.

These five steps usually take about an hour of preparation time, but it's an hour well spent, because we've found it saves us hundreds of dollars each month. We're now feeding a family of four, but when all of our children were at home, we were feeding a family of seven on less money than many smaller families were spending each month. (Our once-a-month major shopping trip usually required two carts and an extra person when we were shopping for seven!) A family that chooses to live with less has to remember that they have more time than money. Taking the time to prepare for shopping assures you of spending less money.

LISTEN

Working together on keeping the grocery budget under control is an important part of a less-is-more family. How can you work together to become smart shoppers? What can you do to help one another with the shopping tasks? Have you ever asked each other those questions and listened carefully to the responses?

Several years ago, we changed our shopping process to accommodate some health challenges Jill was facing. After years of constant pain, she was finally diagnosed with fibromyalgia. The nerves in her body are always on overdrive. This causes pain that eventually wears her out. If she pushes herself physically, her body usually revolts in some way. A full afternoon of grocery shopping was enough to put her out of commission for a couple of days.

Because of this, we brainstormed ideas for new shopping strategies and listened to each other's suggestions. We eventually figured out a new plan that would work for us. Now I time my shopping trips so that Mark and/or my teenagers are available to unload and put away the groceries when I arrive home. If I time it really right, I can sometimes have Mark meet me at the store to transfer the grocery sacks from the cart to the car. And if it's really my lucky day, he'll just shop with me and take care of all the loading, unloading and putting away!

Take the time to think about your "getting ready to shop" strategy. Discuss what steps you currently take and what steps you'd like to expand. Ask each other for ways you can help in the shopping or meal prep process. Listen closely and then respond with a willingness to partner in whatever ways would be helpful.

ADJUST

Making changes in the shopping budget may require adjustment from every member of our family. Several years ago, we discovered the Aldi grocery store. Aldi is a store where you pay for food, not frills or name brands. If you have an Aldi in your neighborhood, it could save you hundreds of dollars. When we began doing the bulk of our shopping at Aldi, I saved an average of $150 each month. But doing so required some adjustment on our part. Whether you have Aldi or another discount, no-frills store that is similar, you might need to make some adjustments like these:

generics

Learning to like generic foods rather than brand-name foods can take a little bit of adjustment. You might start with generic ingredients where the transition isn't as noticeable to the taste buds, and slowly move to include other grocery items. Canned or frozen vegetables, flour, sugar and other staples are basically the same wherever you purchase them. Now we purchase 80 percent of our groceries at Aldi and the generic brands are our new normal.

bags

At discount grocers you sometimes have to bag your own food. For instance, at Aldi, plastic and paper bags are available for purchase. Once we adjusted to keeping grocery bags in our car all the time, we've never had to pay for bags. When you shop at a regular grocery store, you pay for your bags with a few extra cents they add into the price of your products.

carts

Aldi charges a quarter to secure a cart. Don't worry—you get it back at the end of your shopping trip when you return the cart. Discount grocers use strategies like this to keep their staff to a minimum so they can keep their product prices affordable.

Most families who live with less have to adjust to eating at home for the majority of their meals. Recently we were at a social event where several dual-income couples were talking about their favorite restaurants in town. We listened to them talking about their favorite steaks and meals they enjoy on a regular basis. We nodded and contributed where we could to the conversation, but once home we talked about how different our lives are from theirs. The restaurants they eat at regularly are the kinds of places we go to on our anniversary once a year. While we'd love to eat out more often, our commitment to live with less has required us to adjust our expectations and give up some conveniences in exchange for living out our vision for our family.

There have been other adjustments we've also had to make. We don't buy something just because we want it. We eat less junk food, because we've discovered just how much it really costs and how empty the calories really are. We only buy soda pop for special occasions like picnics and birthdays. We've had to adjust to taking more time to prepare for our shopping trip than we had in the past. We're more conscious of buying clothing we need rather than clothing we want. These kinds of adjustments help us to spend less, so we can live with less income, and ultimately focus more on family and relationships rather than working to support a more supersized life.

NAVIGATE

Food: Once we've prepared for our trip, worked together to divide responsibilities, and adjusted our attitudes, it's time to actually shop. After years of sharing and comparing strategies with other families, here are our eight strategies for navigating the grocery-shopping maze:

1. Shop the perimeter. You'll eat healthier and purchase less processed, higher-priced convenience foods if you shop the perimeter of the store first. The perimeter of the store is where you'll find the fresh foods. Shop the aisles only for specific items on your list.

2. Shop high and low. Grocery stores work hard to entice you to impulse shop. Usually they will put more expensive name-brand items at eye level. You'll find your best-buy generic brands on the higher shelves and lower shelves. That also means savvy shoppers can count a shopping trip as their exercise for the day!

3. Eat first. Never go to the grocery store hungry. You're much more likely to buy food you don't need if everything sounds good. If you head out to the grocery store and realize that you haven't eaten, it's worth grabbing a snack before you shop. You'll probably save yourself three to four times the cost of a quick meal by taking care of your hunger before you shop.

4. Purchase sale items in bulk. Most products go on sale in twelve-week cycles. When buying nonperishables that can be stored in a pantry, closet or shelf in the basement, purchase enough to last twelve weeks until the next sale cycle.

5. Shop Alone. You'll be more likely to stick with your list if you shop alone. Make sure, however, that everyone at home is involved in unloading the car and putting the groceries away. They eat, so they can help with food. If a family member needs to be with you, take a few minutes to explain your strategy to them and invite them into the savvy shopping experience. Our kids love helping me when I issue the challenge that we need to get everything on our list at the lowest prices because we have only so much cash to spend. They are equipped with their own calculators, so I have one of them keep a running total of what is in the cart. Another one helps find the best deals by figuring price per pound.

6. Watch for marketing schemes. If something is advertised as "2 for $3," usually it's also "1 for $1.50." Make sure and purchase the number of items you need rather than the number of items they suggest. If you buy in bulk, make sure it really is less money per item. Sometimes bigger isn't better. Sharing bulk purchases with neighbors or friends can help.

7. Shop less often. The less time you are in stores, the less money you will spend. If you can limit your major shopping trips to once or twice a month, you'll find yourself better off. Most of the time even milk can be purchased with an expiration date that is ten to fourteen days out. With our once-a-month shopping trips, we usually make a trip once every ten days or so to get perishables like milk, fresh fruits and vegetables. That trip is limited by a preestablished amount of cash to keep our spending in check.

8. Do meal prep when you come home. We've found that when we take some extra time to prepare some of our meat and fresh fruits and vegetables right after shopping, we eat better and simplify daily meal prep. For instance, if we purchase ten pounds of hamburger at the grocery store, we'll come home and make five pounds into meatloaves and meatballs to freeze. Then we'll brown five pounds of it with a little bit of onion. We'll freeze part of the browned meat in one-pound portions to be used in meals such as chili, stroganoff and spaghetti. We'll season the rest of the browned meat with taco seasoning and then freeze it in one-pound portions to use in enchiladas, tacos and nachos. If it's a late-night grocery trip and we're too weary to brown the meat, we'll sometimes throw it into the Crockpot to cook overnight.

In addition to the meat, if we get the fruit and vegetables ready to eat—cut up cantaloupe, rinse grapes, cut up broccoli and cauliflower, etc.—we're more likely to grab the already prepared fresh food as a quick snack or to add to our meal for dinner.

Once the meal plan is made and the food is purchased, it's time to put the plan to work. The preparation work done up front will make the daily work of feeding the family so much easier. In addition to shopping strategies, wise "living with less" families use some of these food preparation strategies as well:

- One mom we know invited eight friends to participate in a monthly bulk meal exchange. Each mom makes eight identical frozen meals. When they meet each month they bring their frozen meals, all clearly labeled, and distribute them to the other members. Then they each come home with seven completely different meals they didn't have to make!

- Roast two chickens for dinner. Shred the leftover chicken with a fork and freeze in one-pound portions to use in soups or meals like chicken enchiladas, chicken and noodles, or chicken and dumplings. You can do the same with turkey. A large turkey can make half a dozen meals or more.

- Try to incorporate more dried beans, lentils and split peas into your meals. Dried beans are a great, inexpensive and quite filling source of protein.

- Buy seasonal fresh fruits and vegetables. Don't get the precut fruits and veggies—buy them whole and cut them yourself. Get out-of-season produce in the frozen food aisle.
- Create your own snack foods. Repackage things at home when buying in bulk. Cut up your own veggies and put them in smaller-portioned resealable bags. Once a week or every other week, bake cookies and other goodies together as a family. Freeze them for quick on-the-go snacks.
- Don't buy convenience foods. Learn to make cakes, biscuits, pancakes and pasta salads from scratch, because foods made from scratch are usually less expensive. You can even make your own bread crumbs by toasting bread and then putting it in the blender.
- Never throw away leftovers. Keep a plastic container in your freezer to put small amounts of vegetables, meat, soups and such. When the container is full, add tomato sauce and seasonings to make a hearty vegetable soup. You can also use leftover vegetables to create a yummy casserole.
- Buy day-old bread at your local bakery. It usually costs less than the freshest bread.
- Serve a vegetarian meal once or twice a week. This really cuts down on food costs because meat is so expensive.
- Plant a garden and freeze or can anything extra to be used through the fall and winter. If you don't have room for a garden, join a CSA (community-sponsored agriculture) program to get locally grown fresh fruits and vegetables.
- Rather than eating lunch out, take your leftovers to work.
- After Halloween, eat some of your favorite candy and save the rest. Freeze them in small portions until basketball season or some other event you need to take snacks to.
- Plan a soup-and-bread night once a week. This is a filling but inexpensive meal.

- Cook larger portions and put leftovers in the refrigerator so you'll resist going out to a restaurant on a night that you don't have much time.
- When eating fast food, order from the kids' menu. When eating out with your family, require everyone to drink water instead of ordering beverages.
- When you bake breakfast goodies, double or triple the batch and freeze them. You will have a quick breakfast on hand, and it will save you money and keep you from going out to buy something fast on the go.
- Make meal preparation and cleanup a family affair. Everyone in the family eats, so include everyone in both the cooking and the cleaning.

clothing

While the food budget takes up a large part of a family's resources, shopping for clothing can also blow the family budget to smithereens. Adopting some simplifying strategies for clothing our family is absolutely essential for living with less.

Years ago I (Jill) had the opportunity to meet author and speaker Donna Otto. Donna was the first person to introduce me to a truly simple wardrobe. Donna's dark skin and dark hair look great in black. Donna told me that several years earlier she simplified her closet to include only black and white clothing. A splash of red lipstick tops off every outfit. It was a concept I'd never heard of, but her reasoning was solid. Everything in her closet matched. There wasn't one piece of clothing that didn't match. And she had dozens of outfits she could mix and match. Now that's taking simplifying clothing to a whole new level!

While Donna's strategy may be appealing to a few brave folks reading this chapter, my guess is that most of us would rather find simplifying strategies that are a bit more mainstream. With that in mind, here are some strategies for decreasing the family clothing budget:

- Learn to mend clothing rather than discarding it and buying new.
- Build up a basic color scheme of your best colors that can be mixed and matched.
- Build a basic wardrobe of classic clothing. Button-down blouses for women and shirts for men have changed very little over the past ten years.
- Learn to love secondhand stores. Gently used clothing is far easier on the budget.
- Shop out of season when possible. A friend of ours found a great pair of pants at the Gap for $4! Jill found Gap jeans at the same store for $10!
- Yard sales can yield some great children's clothing.
- Be careful about buying clothes just because they are inexpensive. Our friend Beth realized she was doing this. Now she buys only what she loves. She has fewer outfits but she wears what she loves.

Some of us are accustomed to having a closet full of clothes and wearing only a fourth of what's in our possession. Doing a true closet cleanout is refreshing to the spirit and makes clothing selection much simpler. Ask yourself, "Have I worn this in the past year?" If the answer is yes, keep it. If the answer is no, get it out of your closet and out of the house.

It's amazing how much food and clothing can make or break the family budget. The more we think ahead about our preparation and purchases, the more we're able to see less-is-more results. Commit today to trying something new with your family's approach to food. Sometimes even the smallest changes can add up and make a big difference!

Lord, thank You that we have food to eat and clothes to wear. Help us to spend less on convenience foods and focus on having more meals at home and cooked from scratch. We want to be lifelong learners, so help us not to be afraid to learn something new or work to break bad habits. Thank You for what You provide for us. May we never forget just how blessed we are. In Jesus' name, amen.

let's talk about it

This chapter has caused me to think about...

Something I learned in this chapter is...

I am willing to make the following adjustments in order for us to become smart shoppers...

When it comes to food prep, we could...

chapter 13

housing: there's no place like home

SHELTER IS A BASIC NEED. A roof over our head to protect us from the weather is a necessity. But it doesn't need to be a fancy roof, just a sturdy one. It doesn't have to be in an upscale neighborhood; it just needs to be safe. Everyone doesn't have to have her own bedroom, just a bed to sleep on. Wood, brick and siding make a house, but the relationships inside the house make it a home.

Because rent, mortgage and house-related expenses make up so much of our budget, it's important to monitor what we are spending. It's healthy to evaluate our housing expenses annually and ask ourselves if there is anywhere we can cut back or any changes we can make to manage our costs. With a good PLAN in place, we can make sure we're carrying our less-is-more vision into our housing decisions.

PREPARE

Staying on top of housing expenses requires some homework at least every twelve months or so. We've found that when we keep an eye on interest rates, insurance rates, phone plans, propane providers (oh, the joys of living out in the country), and other utilities and services, we're better consumers and money managers. In the same way that a business conducts audits to evaluate the income and expenses of the company, homeowners need to go through a similar process annually to make sure they are getting the most for their money. If you haven't done a housing audit lately, take a look at these expenses and ask yourself if there is anything that you should research thoroughly that could possibly be changed:

- Mortgage/rent. Finance experts suggest this ought to be no more than 25 percent of our take-home pay. What percentage is it for you?
- Could you set up an online payment schedule to pay half of your mortgage every two weeks in order to make one extra mortgage payment a year? Doing this will allow you to take seven years off a conventional thirty-year mortgage.
- Mortgage-interest rate. Could we refinance at a lower rate for a shorter period of time?
- Homeowner's/renter's insurance. Have we shopped rates lately?
- PMI (private mortgage insurance). Have we paid our mortgage down to a point where our home equity is above 20 percent so we can drop PMI?
- Electricity. Could we do an energy audit?
- Trash service. Is there a less expensive service available?
- Property taxes. Could we lower our property taxes if we lived in a different neighborhood?
- Cable/satellite television. Do we need it? Can we downsize our package?
- Phone. Do we need a landline? Could we change long-distance carriers? Should we change cellular carriers? Can we downsize to a package with fewer minutes? Can we do without a data package?
- Internet. Is there a less expensive service provider?

LISTEN

Several years ago we read Willard Harley's book *His Needs, Her Needs*. Eye-opening for us in many ways, Harley's book introduced us to the concept that "financial support" is a basic need of a marriage. Financial support is defined as "knowing the financial plan." Of the ten needs he identifies in the book, financial support is usually in a woman's top five. Regardless of gender, however, when we're talking about anything financial, many emotions, memories, expectations and values are connected to the discussion. Discussing housing options and expenses is no exception.

As you are working through this book, make sure you are listening to the heart of your spouse's communication. Don't jump into defensive mode without affirming to your partner that you have heard her concern. You'll also want to make sure and share ownership of research and changes. If one of you is accustomed to making all the financial decisions, work to unify your efforts and share the responsibility in some way. When we do our annual homeowner audit, we divide the responsibility of the homework and research. This allows both of us to "own" financial responsibility and invest in the process as well as contribute to the solution.

ADJUST

Housing adjustments can be as simple as evaluating the frequency of mortgage payments and as big as choosing to downsize to a smaller home. Our friends the Lebre family made a big housing adjustment. Here's Lori's story in her own words:

> My husband Bob and I were married in 1992. Four years later our first child, Casey, was born. We decided that I should stay home with her during the day, so I changed my work schedule to three evenings a week. I had previously been working full-time. I was nervous that working less would

require me to change my spending habits. We had never lived on a tight budget and always had plenty of money.

When I found out my second child, Kyle, was going to be born with a cleft lip and palate, I began to understand what was really important in life. My faith grew stronger almost every day. It wasn't about me, but what God wanted for my family. After Kyle was born, I just couldn't leave my family three nights a week, so I cut back to two. The less I worked, the more I realized I was spending our money unwisely.

In the summer of 2000, I asked God what He wanted me to do about working because I didn't feel good about my job anymore. My husband was always supportive of my quitting altogether, but I was afraid we'd be too strapped for money. After much prayer, I felt a peace about quitting and I knew that it was the right thing for our family.

Money was tight for the next year, but we were never without and never in debt. However, we still felt we needed to change something.

In the fall of 2004, I began praying for God to help us figure out what we needed to do financially. Moving to a smaller house kept coming to mind. *But nobody does that*, I thought. *Nobody moves to a smaller house! Families move into bigger houses. That's the American way!*

When God finally gave both of us a peace about the possibility of downsizing, we found a smaller house on the opposite side of town. It backed up to the elementary school and was two minutes from our church. It was also four minutes from Walmart, which is where I seem to spend a lot of time as well.

We decided to put an offer on the house. Later that day the house was ours. The same afternoon a couple was driving by our house and saw the FOR SALE sign in our yard.

After walking through our house, they put an offer on it that evening. We basically bought our new house and sold our old house all in one day! We closed on both of the houses three weeks later. It was definitely a God thing!

We downsized and simplified our life dramatically. We have a smaller yard to take care of, less money wasted on bills, less time in the car driving here and there, and less to clean! Our family has found our new perspective and our simplified life is very freeing.

I never thought we'd leave our old house. But when we get right down to it, what is life all about? It's not about the size of your house or yard or what school your kids go to. It's not even about what your family and friends think or say. It's about living your life according to God's plan for your family. It's about being a good steward of what God has given us, living within our means, and realizing we don't need everything the world tells us we need. I have learned that God's view of abundance is not the same as the world's view—it's much better!

The Lebres evaluated their situation and determined that change was necessary. And that change required some work on their part. Sometimes a big change such as downsizing to a smaller home is needed, and sometimes we simply need to make a handful of smaller changes that will add up over time. Adjusting our attitude to cooperate with the change and help with whatever extra work is required is a must.

If a change is needed that will affect you personally, it's very important that you adjust to the new limits. For instance, if both partners determine that a less expensive cable television package is needed, accept the change and adjust to the new programming—without complaining! There's nothing harder on a relationship than agreeing upon changes together and then having one partner remind the other every day of how horrible this idea was. If you choose to move from two incomes to one and you've been accustomed to buying whatever home decoration you wanted, you might just have to learn to like what you have and be content with moving furniture to "redecorate." These attitude adjustments are an important part of living with less. They deepen our relationships with each other, build trust and produce character. Those are some of the "mores" we can experience when we learn to simplify.

NAVIGATE

Everyone handles change differently. Some of us love to change things up. Others are okay with change, but need some time to warm up to new ideas. Still others resist any kind of change. Because our home is very personal to us, keeping these differences in mind is a very important strategy for successfully navigating changes in any area of our family's housing.

One family whose story was shared in a *Woman's Day* article was headed in a direction to make a change and move to a larger house like many of their friends. Rather than upsize from their two-bedroom home, in which their two preteen boys shared a room, however, they finally decided to stay in their small home. She says that "years later, I can say without reservation that this was one of the best decisions we ever made."[12] She goes on to share the many blessings of living in a small home, including the fact that their home is the hangout spot for their boys' friends. She says that proves "that a well-stocked refrigerator trumps extra rooms any day."[13] Stories

[12] Lori Erickson. "The Little House That Could: The big rewards of living small," *Woman's Day*, September 15, 2009: 24.
[13] ibid 26.

like this bolster our courage to battle adult peer pressure and think differently than many other families are thinking. If you're planning on staying in the same home, here are four secrets we've found to making successful changes to our housing expenses.

secret #1

Include the whole family. We all live in the house, so we can all help keep our housing affordable. Motivate the kids to turn the lights off in any room they leave by telling them they'll owe you a quarter anytime they leave a room and don't turn them off. If they're too young to have earning power, start them out with eight quarters, which will be theirs to keep after two weeks as long as they turn out lights during that two-week period. The short-term reward system will help launch new habits that will pay off in the long haul.

secret #2

Little steps can add up to big savings. Weather-strip windows and doors, put on a sweater, and turn down the thermostat. You can also insulate outlets and light switches on outside walls. Minor changes like switching to CFLs (compact fluorescent light bulbs), installing low-flow showerheads, insulating your water heaters and lowering the water heater thermostat to 120 degrees (most are set at 150 degrees) can make a big difference. You can also use cold water for all laundry (except bedding, which needs to be washed in hot to take care of the dust mites), install a programmable thermostat so you can control the temperature throughout the day, and install dimmer switches to turn down the lights when you can. Don't forget to air-dry dishes when you use the dishwasher and unplug appliances that aren't being used (TVs, VCRs, computers, coffeemakers, and other appliances have "phantom electrical loads" that use energy even when they are not fully on). Even planting trees to shade the air-conditioning unit can make a difference. Don't write off making a $20-per-month change just because it doesn't seem like much. Remember that five $20-per-month changes add up to $100 per month and that is a significant savings!

secret #3

When it comes to home decorating, do it yourself as much as possible. When decorating a child's bedroom, choose classic colors and designs rather than buying sheets and decorations of the most recent fad. One mom found that letters spelling out your child's name work well for any age or gender. Another mom discovered that stick-and-remove wall art is an easy and inexpensive way to decorate. Painting, some flooring and landscaping can all be done without a professional. Check out classes at your local home store. If necessary, ask a friend who has more experience than you to help you or show you what to do. You'll not only accomplish your project, but you'll also be able to say, "I did that!"

secret #4

Check out the clearance aisle at your favorite home stores for scratched and dented decorating items that can be freshened up with a coat of paint or a little repair. Paint can also be found on clearance. We've been known to say to one another that "clearance paint is always the right color."

Our home is so much a part of the family experience. It's the place where the family pulls off the highway of life, gathers and finds refreshment. The kind of house, the kind of furniture and the kind of decorating we have are not nearly as important as the kind of relationships inside the home. And keeping the relationship a higher priority than the material is what the less-is-more vision is all about.

Lord, thank You for giving us a roof over our head. Help us to evaluate where our money is going and if there is any way to adjust or change to live with less. We ask for unity in our financial decisions. Help us to be good communicators and good listeners. Show us Your plan for our family, even if it means living with less and doing things differently than the rest of the world. In Jesus' name, amen.

let's talk about it

The one thing that really made me think in this chapter is...

A good time of the year for us to implement a housing audit would be...

After reading the story of the family who downsized, my thoughts were...

I'd like to see us...

chapter 14

transportation: you're driving me crazy

WE ALL HAVE PLACES TO GO AND PEOPLE TO SEE. And that means we all need some way to get where we're going. Next to housing expenses, transportation costs can be the second-largest budget item in a family's spending plan. With car payments, insurance, repairs and fuel, there are plenty of outgoings when it comes to the cost of transportation. Let's take a look at a PLAN for keeping transportation costs under control.

PREPARE

Many times we assume that we need the same number of cars as we have drivers in our family. Every car, however, has its associated expenses, so a family needs to think through this part of their life carefully. The Pankratz family of Rochester, Minnesota, has found that they can make one vehicle work. Mark's brother Jeff and sister-in-law Jacqui, who live in Indianapolis, Indiana, are another one-vehicle family who are making it work so that Jacqui can stay home with their daughter. We, however, live in rural Normal, Illinois, and doing with fewer than two vehicles would be quite challenging for our large family.

Regardless of whether you choose to do one vehicle or two—or three if you have teenagers!—the most important part of preparing is talking. Here are five questions to ask yourself when considering transportation expenses:

1   How many cars do we need? Why?
2   Do we have access to public transportation? Is it possible to use public transportation at all?
3   What about teenagers? What is our position on either providing a vehicle for our teenagers or allowing them to purchase their own vehicle?
4   Can we carpool at all?
5   What alternate forms of transportation can we consider? Biking? Walking?

LISTEN

We all come into family life with our own experiences and precon-ceived notions. Even stopping to evaluate if the family should have one or two vehicles may be a foreign concept to some of us. This is why listening to your partner's thoughts, ideas and concerns is so important. Partners may need to express their fears and take some time to consider an unconventional idea.

We have had to learn how to navigate this discussion. Over the years several of our vehicle discussions have looked something like this:

Mark: The car is going to cost us too much to fix. We need a new one.

Jill: Are you sure it's really more expensive to fix a car we own than to buy a new car?

Mark: I don't want to mess with all of these repairs. It's too much.

Jill: Yes, it's a hassle, I agree. But is it really the wise financial choice? I don't think we can afford a car payment.

Mark: I guess I want what's easiest, but maybe that's not what's most economical.

I had to learn to hear Jill's concerns. My immediate response to a vehicle that was becoming problematic or needed an expensive repair was, "We need a new car." This response would drive Jill nuts, because she felt that I was making a decision and then leaving it up to her to figure out how to pay for it. (I'll admit that there were times that I did that!) Once we started working to hear each other better, we began having healthy conversations about our concerns. Once we both feel heard, then we are able to work together to develop a plan and strategy. There were times the above conversation ended in a decision to fix our current vehicle, even if the repairs were costly. There have been other times that the above conversation ended up with us making the decision to purchase a new, used vehicle. Each time we've tried to listen to each other, value the other person's perspective, and come to a right decision together.

Living with less sometimes requires us to think outside our box. Considering all options is an important part of making these decisions. Learning to have conversations without being too opinionated or defensive has helped us to consider all available options. Keeping in mind that "this isn't a personal thing, it's an economic decision" has been helpful too. Over time, we've communicated better and have therefore made much better decisions.

ADJUST

When the Pankratz family's second car stalled while Angie was on an early-morning trip to the gym, she and her husband Tom soon discovered it was not worth the money to repair it. "We didn't really have the funds to replace it with anything better than a junker," says Angie, "so we decided it was time for us to take a leap of faith and be a one-car family. Angie was actually pregnant with their third child at the time, so they were especially nervous about this, but in time, their decision to live with one car actually brought about some unexpected blessings. In Angie's own words, their top ten blessings include "First, Tom has became very familiar with public transportation. His company actually covers a hundred percent of the cost of his taking the three-mile bus ride to and from work. Second, Tom finds it helpful to have the time on the bus to start his day with Bible reading and prayer. Third, Tom enjoys the trails in the summer to walk or ride a bike to work. He uses this time to pray as well. Fourth, our insurance rates went down as we were only covering one vehicle instead of two. Fifth, our tiny two-car garage now has room for bikes in it. Sixth, we mapped out our errands on Saturdays and did them all together as a family. Seventh, we learned the benefits of carpooling with neighbors who go to the same church as us! Eighth, my husband only had to do half as many oil changes, car washes, etc. Ninth, we felt like we were being more responsible with the earth's resources. And tenth, we found that actually doing with one less car netted our family more time together and even more money because we don't have the expenses associated with another vehicle."

When it comes to keeping transportation costs under control, we sometimes need to adjust from what we want to do to what we need to do. Running errands for half the day on Saturday may not be how you *want* to spend the day, but grouping errands might be a money-saving strategy you *need* in order to save on gas. Getting up early and driving your spouse to work every day, as our sister-in-law Jacqui often does, may not be what you *want* to do, but it might be what you *need* to do in order to have a vehicle available to you during the day. Learning to do your own oil changes may not be what you want to do, but it may be necessary to keep your car-maintenance expenses manageable. Carpooling to work may not be your first choice, but it could be a wise one in order to keep fuel expenses for your family under control. Most of these adjustments qualify as sacrifice, which, if you'll remember from Part 2 of this book, is a much-needed attitude for the less-is-more family to have. The financial margin these types of decisions can provide may very well contribute to the "mores" you want for your family.

NAVIGATE

Once you've decided how to handle your family's transportation needs, you'll need some strategies to keep the costs under control. Place a check mark next to any of these money-saving strategies you'd like to put into practice:

- Explore public transportation.
- Evaluate auto-insurance premiums.
- Be more proactive about maintaining vehicles. (If we ignore maintenance and small repairs, the result is likely more expensive repairs.)
- Explore carpooling opportunities for work or school.
- Be more intentional about grouping errands.
- Consider doing with one less vehicle.

Another tool many families use for navigating transportation is a "driving contract" for teenage drivers (you can Google "teenage driving contract" to find samples of agreements other families have used). It has been helpful for our family to physically spell out the responsibilities and financial obligations of driving. In our family, if teenagers are going to drive, they have to share in the costs of driving (gas, insurance, oil changes, etc). Having a tool to spell out those expectations has helped keep costs under control and expectations clear. We've also found that one of the easiest ways for teenage drivers to contribute to keeping the costs of auto insurance under control is to get good enough grades to qualify for the good-student discount. We spell out in our contract that if they don't have good grades, they will have to pay their portion of the premium plus the difference between the good-student discount and their premium. If they can't pay, they can't drive.

Other strategies that successful less-is-more families use include:

- Utilizing car-maintenance coupons, such as free or discounted oil changes found in the newspaper or in coupon books, or by getting on the preferred-customer mailing list of a local quick-change company.

- When buying a car, negotiate the price and then negotiate the value of your trade-in. This keeps the dealer from using your trade-in to determine the price of your new car.

- Explore financing options before you buy a car so you are not dependent on auto-dealer financing. Sometimes bank loans or credit-union loans are at lower interest rates than dealer financing.

- To save money on premiums, raise your deductible. Just make sure you have the deductible amount in savings in case you need to use it.

- When you finish making payments on a car, keep making the payment into a "future car" savings account. Then pay cash for your next car!

- Don't buy premium fuel. The average car can handle the less expensive gas just fine.
- Slow down. Driving ten miles per hour above sixty-five is like adding seventy-four cents to the price of a gallon of gas.[14]
- Rotate your tires every six months and check the pressure monthly.
- Buy used vehicles. New cars depreciate by the thousands the minute you drive them off the lot. (For a small fee, you can research the VIN—Vehicle Identification Number—at www.carfax.com. You can also find good information about cars at www.autos.msn.com and www.kbb.com.)
- If you buy new, plan to drive your car for seven to ten years. With good maintenance, cars can last at least this long.
- Beware of leasing a car. While it can be right in some situations, you have a perpetual car payment and never own the car.
- Buy for gas mileage and safety, not style or color.

It's necessary for us to have the ability to get from one place to another. But it's not necessary for us to do it the way that everybody else does. Are you starting to grasp the power of peer pressure in the adult world? Unfortunately, it doesn't really stop after the teen years. But many times we don't recognize what it is. Think through your family's transportation needs, your financial picture, and make the decisions that are right for your less-is-more family.

---

[14] Alice Garbarini Hurley, "Drive Down Your Car Costs," *Good Housekeeping*, September 2008: 109.

Lord, we need Your wisdom. Show us how to evaluate our transportation needs wisely. Help us to discuss it openly and to find middle ground from what may be differing perspectives. We want to live with less, but that may mean we have to live differently than our family, friends and neighbors. Help us to not worry about what other people think and to focus only on how You are leading our family to live. In Jesus' name, amen.

let's talk about it

This chapter caused me to really think about...

In the Navigate section, I'd like for us to put these money-saving strategies in place...

What will be/is our philosophy on teenagers and driving?

chapter 15

holidays: santa's on a budget and vacation is a nonnegotiable

EVERY FAMILY NEEDS AN OPPORTUNITY TO GET AWAY FROM THE EVERYDAY. A break in routine is a necessity for emotional health, physical health and relational health. The holidays give us a regular schedule for taking a break, spending time with family, and giving the body and mind the rest it needs. In addition to the holidays, a well-planned vacation provides an extended time of rest and relaxation. But holidays, celebrations and vacation don't have to cost a lot of money; they just needs to be approached with some thoughtful intentionality. Let's look at some effective strategies to PLAN vacation and holiday time for your family.

PREPARE

Ten years ago, Jill's parents sold the family farm and bought a condo in Florida. They don't live there—it's an investment and a convenient vacation spot for them as well as for their three daughters and our families.

Almost annually, our family makes the trek to Florida for a week of rest, relaxation and fun in the sun. Several years ago, a summer family wedding in Colorado kept us from our Florida fun. When Jill suggested that we take a side trip to Yellowstone Park, the kids (and Mark) revolted with, "Hey, that's not a vacation. That's a field trip!" Oh, the joys of trying to please seven people.

In a way, though, Mark and the kids were right: Our vacations at the beach are very relaxing. But when I (Jill) was growing up, my family took field trips for vacations. We explored the Grand Canyon, Yellowstone, Mackinac Island, and Washington, DC. We stayed in campgrounds, setting up our six-person tent each night. And our kids really haven't had that same experience. We've stopped at museums and civil-war sights on our way to Florida, and we have explored other parts of the country at times, but there are still some "field trips" that would be worthwhile to take our family on.

What we've learned, though, is that the timing of these experiences is vital because exploring Washington, DC, with a three-year-old is not anyone's idea of fun. What we decided to do many years ago was to prepare a plan—a schedule for vacations (aka "field trips") when our family members were at optimal ages to enjoy the destinations. This three-step process not only helped us set some goals for the travel and experiences we wanted to have with our family, but it also helped us consider the financial boundaries for these endeavors and inspired us to intentionally save toward our goals.

1. have a brainstorming session

The first step we took in creating our schedule was to brainstorm. We used one of our date nights to talk about places we'd been as a child or places we'd never been but wish we had. We discussed experiences we wanted our kids to have while they were still at home. We dreamed about places we'd love to visit ourselves.

2. create a table

This proved to be a bit emotional for Jill. We created a table that listed each year and the ages of our kids that particular summer. She found herself tearing up as she realized the small number of years we really had with our children at home.

3. match our dreams with reality

Living on a limited income, we could only take a major trip every two to three years, so we whittled our list down to what we could realistically afford. We then plugged the trip into our table according to when our children would be at the appropriate ages to enjoy it to the fullest. And then we began to work on our plan, saving money and researching the experience so we could really maximize the fun while minimizing our budget.

While this process hasn't been foolproof, it has given us a definite advantage in accomplishing our goals. Our well-planned once-in-a-lifetime trip to Disney World, which we took when our kids were sixteen, fourteen, twelve and six, was so much fun. But the following year we added a nine-year-old son to our family through adoption. He still has not been to Disney World, and every once in a while he politely reminds us of that. While it's certainly not something we owe him, it is something we'd love for him to experience, so now we've discussed adding a second trip to Disney into our vacation plan for the future.

This strategy works with any type of experience you'd like to do with your family—or even as a couple. It doesn't have to cost a lot of money or be a trip to Disney. There are many great opportunities in your own backyard—museums, historical sites, zoos, bed-and-breakfasts, maybe even a train trip somewhere. But those experiences are best enjoyed when the kids are at just the right ages and stages of life.

Do you dream about experiences you'd like to have with your family? Would you like to maximize the time you have with your kids and strategize about the experiences you want to offer them? Would you like to do something special as a couple? Then grab a piece of paper and start talking, listening, dreaming and planning today, because as Jill's friend Charlene says, "Don't miss your kids—they'll be gone before you know it!"

Holiday planning can look somewhat similar. Ask yourself, "What do we want to accomplish with our holiday time together?" Holidays can be vacation time and it can simply be an opportunity to get together with friends or extended family. It's important to remember, however, that only you know what is best for your family. Don't let extended family expectations (i.e., adult peer pressure) pressure you into a cross-country road trip you can't afford or a weekend with family members you'd rather not spend a lot of time with. You and your spouse must determine how your family will spend the holidays. And planning ahead is key to making and communicating those decisions before you're in the midst of the holiday season.

Another part of the Christmas holiday that deserves a plan has to do with gift giving. What is your budget for each child? How are you going to handle gift exchanges with extended family? What parameters do you need to set financially so that you will stay on budget and focus on the time with family more than the gift giving? These kinds of questions are best answered months before the holiday season. A decision made well in advance can help you stick to your guns when the Christmas music and holiday decorations tempt you to forgo your well-thought-through plans.

LISTEN

When it comes to being emotionally refueled, every one of us is different. Mark is an extrovert who is refueled by being with people. Jill, on the other hand, is an introvert, which means she is refueled by being alone. Mark likes the beach and doing nothing. Jill likes to do nothing, but she also likes to explore. So what are two opposites supposed to do for holidays and vacations? Well, just like every other area in which we're different, we have to learn to compromise.

As holidays are approaching, it's important to ask each other:

- What would you like Christmas vacation to look like?
- How do you want your time with extended family to look during Thanksgiving? Remember, you can choose when and how much time you'll spend with extended family. You may not be on your mother-in-law's happy list, but you and your spouse are the only ones who can determine what is best for your immediate family.
- What do you want to do with the Fourth of July vacation day you'll have in the summer?
- Let's plan an overnight getaway for just you and your spouse this summer. What would your dream twenty-four-hour getaway look like?
- What can we do to transform gift giving during the Christmas season for the family?
- What can we give or do for birthdays and other celebrations that doesn't cost a lot of money?

ADJUST

Many of us would love to live the resort life on vacation every year. When you choose to live with less, you're likely giving up some of those kinds of dreams. But remember, you are exchanging them for more time with family in general, more patience, more margin and less stress in everyday life. In fact, you may need resort life less because your stress level decreases so much. However, you'll still need some kind of break from everyday life. We all do.

Another adjustment that pertains to the holidays applies to gift giving. If you've been accustomed to getting all of your birthday, graduation and Christmas gifts at the store, you'll need to think a little harder. Living with less means giving with less. The gifts aren't less meaningful, but they are less expensive and may require a bit more time.

We need to adjust expectations so we're excited about what can happen rather than disappointed about what can't. Even if your only vacation option is a staycation—to use the recent coinage for a vacation enjoyed at home—there is still so much to enjoy and do during a week off. When your Christmas gift to your sister is a framed picture of the two of you at a family gathering (picture and frame from Walmart) rather than the tennis bracelet she had on her list, you'll find a sense of pride and accomplishment of giving her something so personal and unique. We are only limited by our attitude and our creativity. Let it flow!

NAVIGATE

Too often we allow ourselves to get sucked into the "consumer" mindset of a vacation or a holiday. The most important strategy for navigating holidays and vacations is to remember who and what it is we're celebrating. When we redefine priorities, spending time *with* people becomes much more important than spending money *on* people. To navigate this transition, let's look at some ways we can rethink and re-create what we do for vacations and celebrations.

vacations

Getting away from the everyday is important for us individually and as a family unit. We need time to rest and time to play, especially without the distractions of phone, e-mail and video games. But vacations don't have to cost a lot of money. The best way to start planning is by talking with God about your desire for a vacation. Ask Him for creativity that works within your price range.

Some families vacation at home with what many are calling a staycation—stepping away from everyday routines and planning a week of vacation while sleeping at home every night. One family's staycation looked like this: On Monday they drove one hour to their state capital to visit the state museum, packing a picnic lunch and dinner and enjoying the meals in two different parks. Tuesday featured a one-and-a-half-hour drive to visit a local Amish community and eat in an Amish home. On Wednesday, they chose to stay home and watch movies all day, eating the food they'd purchased in the Amish community as well as popcorn, nachos and other junk foods they rarely have. On Thursday, they ventured to the local zoo, picnicked in the park, and visited their favorite ice cream shop. They finished out their week on Friday with a full day spent at the local pool. Both parents reported that they felt refreshed by their creative vacation and that their family benefited from the intentional time spent together for a week. A staycation takes some self-discipline. Plan to keep away from the phone, e-mail and even regular household chores.

Another option is a long weekend getaway that requires fewer hotel nights than a weeklong vacation. A weekend getaway visiting friends and family who don't live too far away can also make for some much-needed time of rest and relaxation. Other strategies for saving money include an Internet search of "free things to do in Chicago" or whatever city you are visiting. You can also visit the city's visitor's bureau or chamber of commerce Web site for more ideas of free or affordable things to do. Don't forget to look online for "free admission" days at museums. It's also a good idea to vacation in places that aren't the usual hot spots. Rather than going to Orlando or Miami, try Mexico Beach, Florida. Never heard of it? Most people haven't, but such cities and towns are often the best-kept secrets in many parts of the country.

Vacationing out of season can be another money-saving strategy for a getaway. This works great before the kids are enrolled in school.

When we homeschooled our kids, we could vacation any time of the year. Even families whose children are in school have been known to take a week off during the school year to take advantage of a less expensive vacation. The panhandle of Florida is absolutely beautiful in September and October, but their peak summer-vacation season only runs through August. You'll find better prices if you can vacation out of season.

We've also found that the Priceline.com Web site has completely transformed our hotel accommodations. We've stayed at the Hyatt Regency in a Chicago suburb for $25 a night. On another trip we stayed at the Doubletree Chicago for $35 a night. It's been more than five years since we paid full price for a hotel room, thanks to the "name your own price" program at Priceline. (If you use this, just be aware that when you bid on your room, if your bid is accepted you are actually pre-purchasing your hotel room. No refunds. Make sure you really are going on this trip!) Our family has used this for years and on average we pay $35 for a hotel room!

Some families have found camping an inexpensive getaway option. You can borrow, rent or buy some basic camping equipment and enjoy the great outdoors. We have a "vintage"—some would just say it's old—camper that we sometimes loan out to family and friends. Don't be afraid to ask friends or family who might be able to help you out with camping equipment to successfully get away. You just might receive!

Our favorite camping location is just fifteen miles from our home at a campsite right on a lake. Sitting around the campfire, listening to the crickets, and watching the sun set over the water drains away the cares of the day. It doesn't matter that we're still so close to home. It feels as if we're a million miles away.

Vacations by car are usually less expensive than flying. Some families have taken flying somewhere completely out of their reality. Instead, they've capitalized on the family time in the car. After all, it's a little difficult to sing "the wheels on the bus go round and round" on an airplane! It's those kinds of moments that less-is-more families are really looking for anyway.

Our family travels almost exclusively by car. When we travel, we pack sandwiches, snacks and a cooler of drinks to have in the car. We make it our goal to buy nothing but gas on the road. On the rare occasion when we eat out, we prepare the kids to share restaurant meals and drink water with their meals to save money. Think about it: The average price for restaurant drinks is now $2 a person. For a family of five, that's an additional $10 added to the bill.

celebrations

Birthday celebrations are a perfect time to honor each person in a unique way. We usually begin a birthday celebration by telling the story of the person's birth (or adoption)—after all, everyone loves to hear a story about themselves! After waking up to a decorated room, the honored person in our family enjoys cake and ice cream for breakfast, and then the family goes around the table and everyone shares two things that we appreciate about the birthday boy or girl. Words of encouragement are a powerful gift.

One family we know watches home videos of the birthday person together. The shared laughter and memories are beautiful gifts that cost only time, not money.

To manage birthday-celebration expenses, some families limit the number of parties their kids have. Some friends of ours have the tradition of having a family birthday party on even birthdays and having a friend birthday party on odd birthdays. While most families include tangible gifts as part of the birthday celebration, most living-with-less families have a limited, preset budget to keep in mind.

Family-wedding celebrations and gift giving can also be done in a simple, tradition-honoring way that doesn't cost much money. One creative gift is family recipes. A recipe box or book filled with the family's favorite recipes is a wonderful shower or wedding gift. Sit down and go through your recipe box and pull out your family's favorite recipes. Take time to copy each recipe on a new recipe card and place it in the appropriate category in the book or box. This gift will not only encourage the new couple in their kitchen, but may also start a tradition that can be passed down through the years.

Another gift for the bride or groom that takes time but no money is a birthday list. Up until adulthood, a child depends on his or her parents to alert them when it's Grandma's birthday or a brother and sister-in-law's anniversary. Once they're on their own, the responsibility to remember birthdays and anniversaries is theirs. If you type up a list of the family birthdays and anniversaries and give it as a gift, they'll be equipped to remember important family dates with a card or a phone call. If you want to go one step further, contact his or her future mother-in-law and get the dates for that side of the family as well. Accompanied by a box of "all occasion" cards, this can be a thoughtful and affordable gift.

Do you have decorations or celebration supplies you've used throughout the years? At my wedding shower, my mother gave me a box of cake-decorating supplies—some new and some old. Another mom I know gave her daughter a "Happy Birthday" banner they had used in their home. Fill a box with celebration items that were used throughout his or her childhood. This gift starts the newlyweds with some celebration supplies of their own.

Another low-cost gift idea is a box of personal Christmas decorations. A new husband and wife start off without much in the way of Christmas decorations. A shoebox filled with their handmade or personalized ornaments you've collected over the years will allow them to bring a homespun touch to their new Christmas traditions. Our family has the tradition of giving our children a Christmas ornament every year. By the time the older three married, they each had about twenty ornaments we were able to wrap up and give them as a wedding gift.

Speaking of Christmas traditions, if we're going to navigate outside the box for holiday celebrations, we'll have to start with defining the real reason for the holiday. With that definition clear in our minds, then you can get those creative juices flowing. Sometimes creating a new normal for your holiday traditions helps your family keep the main thing the main thing. These new traditions can make the holiday more significant and far less expensive.

For Easter, the focus on Jesus' sacrifice for us should be central to our celebration. We established that early on for our kids, and they never associated Easter baskets, candy, toys and a bunny with Easter at all. Many families observe Lent for the forty days leading up to Easter, talking about the sacrifice that Christ made on the cross and asking each family member to "sacrifice" something as a way to make Easter more meaningful.

Some families decorate eggs together and use the time to talk about the real Easter story. Others use the days leading up to Easter to read the Easter story together at dinner or bedtime (you'll find it in Luke chapters 23 and 24). When the kids were young, we shared the Easter story by using plastic eggs. Each egg contained a specific item and a Bible verse that help tell the Easter story. We numbered the eggs and then allowed the kids to open one egg each day in order. This helps us to tell the Easter story in a creative way. It is especially beneficial to those kids who best learn with hands-on activities. Here are the items:

#9	Cracker	Mark 14:22
#8	Three dimes	Matthew 26:14–15
#7	Thorn	Mark 15:17
#6	Two sticks (to make a cross)	John 19:16–17
#5	Nail	Luke 23:33

#4	White cloth	Matthew 27:57–60
#3	Stone	Matthew 27:49–60
#2	Cinnamon sticks (burial spices)	Mark 16:1
#1	Empty	Mark 16:5–6

As our kids have aged we've watched the *Jesus* movie or *The Passion of the Christ* together as a family (make sure your children are the appropriate age to view these). Easter doesn't have to cost a dime to celebrate. It's about the beautiful story of Jesus' death and resurrection that opened up the possibility of eternity with God. Keeping that at the center of the celebration keeps the priorities in the right place.

Thanksgiving is a holiday most often associated with family gatherings. While there aren't gifts to give, we can still get our priorities mixed up. When we host Thanksgiving for our extended family, Jill has to remind herself that this celebration isn't about the perfect meal and the perfect house. It's about our imperfect family coming together to press the pause button on life and consider all we have to be thankful for.

Some families go around the table and ask everyone to share one thing they are thankful for. One family we know makes their prayer before the Thanksgiving meal one that everyone participates in. Another family hosts a pitch-in Thanksgiving meal that everyone contributes to. And if you want to do something completely different, sign up the whole family to serve Thanksgiving dinner at your local soup kitchen.

The Christmas holiday season can be one of the toughest challenges for living-with-less families. Whether it's decorating, gift giving or navigating family gatherings, the call of culture is so strong. But there are families who successfully celebrate the Christmas holiday in a simple, yet meaningful way. In the Ehman family, each child has three gifts under the Christmas tree. This represents the three wise men, who each brought a gift to the baby Jesus; one gift for the body, one for the mind, and one for the soul can work well. The Nesby family has a birthday party for Jesus, complete with cake and ice cream. Our family has read the Christmas story aloud from the Bible on Christmas Eve or Christmas morning. We've participated in Samaritan's Purse (www.samaritanspurse.com) and Operation Angel Tree (www.angeltree.org) to make Christmas more about giving than receiving. We're also starting to join the ranks of families who are transitioning from traditional gift giving to giving gifts of hope that help families around the world find their way out of poverty. If you'd like to learn more about these opportunities, check out organizations like the Heifer Project (www.heifer.org), World Vision (www.worldvision.org), and Compassion International (www.compassion.com). When we do this, our willingness to have less will actually give another family more. Now that's an exciting benefit of redefined priorities!

When thinking about redefining gift giving, here are some suggestions that have worked from other less-is-more families.

- Set a budget based upon how much you have put into a Christmas account during the year. Predetermine how much money you'll spend on each family member. Put cash in envelopes with the person's name on it.
- Begin thinking about Christmas gifts in July. This gives you enough time to watch for sales and make as many gifts as possible with the same budget.
- Celebrate with extended family the week after Christmas and take advantage of the post-Christmas sales.
- Make your own gifts (a tree ornament, homemade bread, a tin of cookies, a box of fudge, stamped note cards, etc.)
- If you have a hobby like photography, poetry, woodworking or painting, make personalized gifts for friends and family.

- Give words of encouragement. Write a thoughtful card to someone. Write and frame a tribute to a family member or close friend.

Part of what makes a house a home is the way the family celebrates together. Those celebrations often form traditions. And the traditions are an anchor to our sense of family identity. Because our culture often equates celebrations with spending money, we have to be willing to think differently. Redefining priorities is really about thinking differently. Commit today to rethink, redefine and refine your vacation and celebration mindset.

Lord, when You created this earth, You worked for six days and rested on the seventh day. Thank You for creating both work and rest. Help us to find that balance in our lives. We also pray that we would see our opportunities rather than our limitations. Give us both creativity and discipline to provide times of rest and recreation for our family. When it comes to holidays and celebrations, Lord, help us to focus on who and what we are celebrating. Keep our minds protected from the influences of culture that drag us into consumerism. We want to live a simpler, less expensive life that truly provides more for our relationships. In Jesus' name, amen.

let's talk about it

Reading this chapter caused me to realize . . .

I'd like to suggest that we rethink or re-create this holiday celebration . . .

I have these ideas for re-creating our vacation mindset . . .

chapter 16

college: higher education at lower cost ———————

IF YOU WANT TO KNOW ONE SAVAGE PARENT-
ING REGRET, just ask us about our experience leading our older
children through college. We're still apologizing to Anne and Evan
for our mistakes along the college journey. Bottom line: We didn't
discuss this issue early enough in our marriage. By the time we really
talked about it, Anne was embarking upon college with very little
financial leadership from us. Both she and Evan have thousands of
dollars of school loans they (and their spouses) are now paying off.
We've learned a lot of lessons over the past seven years. Our hope is
that you won't make the same mistakes we did. In order to do that,
let's look at a PLAN for leading our children through the maze of
higher education.

PREPARE
prepare your hearts

We both wanted our children to have a traditional college experience. Go to college. Live in the dorm. Make memories. Get a
degree. That's what we had our hearts set on. But there are several
obstacles to that plan. First, we have to have the money to make
that happen. And we don't have that. Honestly, even if both of us
had worked full-time for the past twenty-five years of parenting,

we probably wouldn't have the money to send five children to the colleges of their choice. That's reality. Second, we have to prepare our hearts to adjust to our kids' desires for higher education or career training. Not every kid is wired for college or the traditional go-to-college-right-after-high-school experience. Some may flourish at a trade school or a technical program. A community college might be just right for others. One might do better to take a break after high school, work for a year or two, and then pursue a college degree. Some might want to do something bigger than themselves, like volunteering for the Peace Corps. Still others might want to consider the military. There is no one-size-fits-all picture. So we have to prepare our hearts for our children to have a different picture of their futures than we might have for them. We have to be willing to listen to each child's vision even if it's different from ours.

prepare financially

We were not prepared financially for our children's college education. Mark didn't finish his college degree until after our third child was born. We were paying his college bills for many years and couldn't even think about saving for our kids' degrees. If your children are young, even saving a small amount from each paycheck could make a difference, especially with compound interest on your side.

prepare your child

It's important that we help our children begin thinking about their futures realistically. Good grades and excellence in sports or the arts may lead to scholarships. Working a summer job during high school will allow for several years of savings. Considering all the options available is also valuable, such as trade school, working for a year or two after high school, enlisting in the military, going to a less expensive junior college or community college for the first two years. Not everyone graduates from high school and goes on to the college of his or her choice. In fact, in these challenging economic times, it's happening less often than in the past. But we as parents have to lead our kids to understand all of the options available to them as well as their responsibility in making that happen. We're also preparing our younger children for the reality that because we've been committed to living on a limited income so that we could provide more while they were growing up, we cannot pay for their education. They'll need to pay for it themselves. However, we're also leading them to understand how they might be able to do that without taking out a student loan. We'll talk about that in the Navigate section of this chapter.

LISTEN

Discussing our higher education dreams for our children can be very challenging. We certainly found it to be difficult. The biggest reason is that we came from very different experiences.

Mark was on his own for higher education. He wishes he'd had more leadership from his parents. He would have liked more help discovering and thinking through options for college and college funding. It didn't bother him that he had to pay for his own college, but rather that he had no assistance in navigating life after high school.

Jill was able to go to the college of her choice, and her parents paid for it fully. That was a good experience for her and she wanted to offer that same experience to our children. What she failed to consider, however, is that Mark's earning power in the ministry was not the same as her father's as a school administrator. She also failed to take into consideration that when she was in late grade school, her parents inherited a good sum of money from a relative who had passed away. They invested that money in a college fund for her and her two sisters. And the third thing she failed to consider is that her folks had three children, while we have five. That's a major difference! So even though Jill wanted the same thing for our kids, we simply have not had the resources to make that happen.

Talking through our different experiences, different hopes and different desires for our kids was not easy. And because we weren't in unity, we didn't lead them well. Here are some questions to get you and your spouse talking:

- What was your experience with higher education?
- What would you like to offer your children for post high-school education?
- What if your child has a different vision than college? How do you feel about the military? Peace corps? Trade school? Working for a year or two?
- What can you financially offer your child for a college education?
- What steps should you be taking to prepare your children for post high-school options?

Looking back on our early—but very late-in-the-game—conversations, what we realize is that we weren't listening to each other well and we also weren't moving from our disagreeing points of view into a strategy we could agree upon together. Listen carefully and let your spouse know that you hear him or her, but make sure to find a higher-education strategy that you can agree upon and carry out.

ADJUST

When Jill's girlfriend answered the phone, she could tell something was very wrong. "What's wrong?" Jill asked, forgetting the original reason for her phone call.

"I just got off the phone with the college our daughter wants to go to next year," her friend sobbed, "and we don't qualify for hardly any financial aid. It looks like she won't be able to go to the college she wants to."

The biggest adjustment we found that we needed to make is in coming to terms with the death of a dream. We all want to make our children's dreams come true. When reality clashes with dreams, there is a wide range of emotions we'll experience. Disappointment. Anger. Regret. Sadness. The sooner we can face our reality, the easier it will be to accept what we can't do and begin to look at what we can do. And the sooner we face our reality, the better we can lead our children.

If your income bracket will allow you to finance college, then let your kids know their limits. If you've been able to save money in, say, a prepaid tuition program that allowed you to lock in tuition prices at any in-state college, then let your kids know that they can go to any college within the state lines. If you've saved a little and can help them but not fully pay for college, let them know what you can do and what they have to be responsible for. And if you can't help them financially at all, lead them well, help them know their options, cast vision for scholarships, and teach them to manage their money throughout high school and college so they can pay their own way through school. Whatever your circumstances, adjust to them, accept them, and then work within them.

NAVIGATE

In the living-with-less family, the "more" you can give your children isn't about money. You're giving them more time, more leadership, more laughter, more availability and more attention. So when it comes to navigating post-high school choices, bring them all the "more" you can.

Talk through your options. What about student loans? They are often considered a necessity to obtain a college education. And they may be right for some situations. What we've wanted to do with this book, however, is to help you think differently. To consider other options. To explore other strategies to secure a college degree. Small school loans may not be a big deal to pay off after college, but larger amounts of debt could cripple a young couple or even prohibit them from being able to live their own less-is-more life due to the debt load they are carrying. Mary Hunt offers a helpful tool on her Web site (www.cheapskate.com) to offer some guidance for how much debt is okay for the type of job the degree will prepare the student for. If you are considering student loans, this is a good resource to check out.

Some families have used a 529 savings plan to save for college. A 529 is an education-savings plan operated by a state or educational institution and it's designed to help families set aside funds for future college costs. Most 529 plans have great tax benefits. Every state has different guidelines for 529 accounts, so just make sure you know and understand both the benefits and limitations of the plan in your state.

Also have your child check with the school and the local newspaper at least twice a month for scholarship opportunities. Many local scholarships are not used or applied for; they may be small, but they add up. They are often based on different qualifications—not always academic scores—and may require community service or achievement in a particular field (sports, the arts). In your research, however, be sure to watch out for grant scams. You should never pay anyone to help you with college financial aid.

You should also check out www.upromise.com. It allows you to save for college by doing things like shopping online, using credit cards, going to the grocery store, etc. Once registered, each purchase with a Upromise partner puts a percentage of your purchase in your child's Upromise account.

One other suggestion to consider is the military. With the GI Bill and other educational benefits, a stint in the military can cover the full cost of a bachelor's or graduate degree. We've been learning quite a bit about educational benefits for those who serve in the military lately. Our newest son-in-law has joined the Army. While he has to commit to four years of active service and four years of reserve service, he has the ability to get a bachelor's degree and a master's degree at nearly no cost. He may be able to do part of his education while actively serving, or he can wait until his four years are over and then go to school full-time. Some educational benefits extend to his wife, who now also qualifies for a military discount at some colleges and universities. Serving in the military certainly has an element of risk to it, but it also has quite a few educational benefits to consider. If your son or daughter has interest in enlisting, do your homework, ask questions, and don't be afraid to encourage that endeavor.

We've been doing the "college thing" for the past six years. We describe our experience as a ride up a steep learning curve; in a sense, we've had to go to school ourselves to better understand the options available. Here are 5 School Strategies we've identified for less-is-more families:

1   Always fill out the FAFSA. This is the online application for determining federal and state financial aid at any school. If your income is lower, then you may qualify for more scholarships and grants. This is where your "less" could become a "more!" Fair warning, however: Middle-income

families rarely qualify for much aid beyond student loans. We did find, though, that our income level usually qualifies our kids for work study, which gives them first priority for on-campus jobs. The FAFSA also may qualify your student for state grants you aren't even aware of. Every little bit helps.

2   Consider community college for two years. This makes the first two years of college so much more affordable. Our two oldest kids went to private colleges with tuition of approximately $12,000 per semester. Neither one completed degrees at the private college, because of the money. Our third child is currently attending community college at the price of $88 per credit hour—a total of $1320 per semester. She will complete her associate's degree next year after spending just $5,280 on all four semesters of tuition! We paid for her first semester of college because she was a homeschooled high-school student. (She actually finished high school at the community college and got both high school and college credit at the same time!) She has paid cash for the remaining semesters from money she saved through high school as well as the part-time jobs she has carried through college.

3   Consider state schools to finish a bachelor's degree. After community college, the less expensive option for the remaining two years is a state school. The average state school costs about $12,000 per year (before housing), which is about $350 to $400 per credit hour. The average private college tuition is $23,000 per year (again, without housing), or about $850 per credit hour.

4   Motivate your students to get good grades and ACT/SAT scores. Even if not the class valedictorian, your son or daughter may be able to qualify for some academic

scholarships based upon grade point average or standardized test scores. Our daughter Anne's GPA qualified her for a $2,000-per-year academic scholarship. Sure, that was a drop in the bucket given the $24,000-per-year tuition, but it was something! Our daughter Erica also discovered that if we lived in the next county over, her ACT score would have qualified her for a full scholarship to the local community college. Too bad that the college in our county didn't offer the same kind of academic scholarship, but this illustrates that every college is different and you have to do your homework.

5   Teach money management to your children. This will serve them well throughout college and the rest of their lives. Children don't learn to manage their money by osmosis; they learn by what we teach them directly. Once your child/teenager has any sort of earning power, give him guidance on how to manage his money. Help him to think through what he needs to be saving toward (car, auto insurance, college, etc.) and how each paycheck should be divided so he is saving as well as pulling out cash to spend. We also teach our kids that they need to reserve 10 percent of each paycheck to give to God. This way they are learning to give, save and spend wisely.

All parents want to give their children the best opportunities: lessons, sports, teams, schools and at some point a higher education. But like every other part of a less–is–more life, we have to be willing to adjust our expectations and possibly think differently about post-high school education. An education is very important, but doing it in a way that meshes with your family's vision is equally important.

Lord, we want so much for our children. But we also know that just like we can't have it all, they can't have it all either. It's okay for them to know their boundaries and learn to work within them. Help us to determine what we can do for college. Give us compassion and sensitivity in our discussions on the subject. Help us find unity in a strategy and direction that we can use to lead our kids. In Jesus' name, amen.

let's talk about it

After reading this chapter I have come to realize . . .

When it comes to preparing our kids for post-high school opportunities, I'd like to see us . . .

chapter 17

income: make money doing what you love

IN THE TWENTY-THREE YEARS OF OUR COMMIT-
MENT TO LIVE WITH LESS IN ORDER TO GIVE OUR
FAMILY MORE, Mark has been the primary financial provider
for our family. But he hasn't been alone in that endeavor. Jill contributes greatly to our income in two different ways. First, by saving
us money—Jill covers childcare, meals and housework. She uses her
time to shop carefully and stays on top of our money management.
Her savings alone could come close to providing the equivalent of
a second income to our family. But there's a second way that Jill
contributes to our income. And that's with a home business.

As Jill sat down to write this chapter, it forced her to think about
all the different ways she has brought income into the family while
staying home. She has:

- Sold Avon products.
- Taught piano and voice lessons in our home.
- Served as a wedding musician.
- Been a hired accompanist for school choirs and contests.
- Operated a home day care.
- Worked as a part-time director of women's ministry at our
  church—a job she accepted with a requirement that she be
  able to do the job completely from home.

- Done family photography—a hobby that sometimes brings in a little income.
- Become known as an accomplished speaker.
- Written books and articles for families.

Some things Jill has been able to do with our children in tow, like selling Avon in the neighborhood and running a day care. Others, like accompanying, performing for weddings, and photography, she has done on nights and weekends when Mark is home. Still others she was not able to do until the kids were older—for instance, her first book wasn't written until they were all in school. It would have been impossible when they were small.

If you'd like to have one parent home full-time or part-time but the savings side of things isn't quite enough to make the economics work, consider a home business to fill in the financial gap. With a good PLAN in place, you can succeed in finding a second income without ever having to actually *go* to work.

PREPARE

The most successful home-business owners are the ones who do something they love. In order to assess what you might be able to do, ask yourself these questions:

- What do you enjoy doing?
- What talents do you have that others would pay for?
- What are people always asking you to help them with?
- What products do you believe in so much that you are always telling other people about them?
- What services do my neighbors need? Dog walking? Lawn mowing? Provision of meals for working parents?

The answers to these questions can help you discover what you enjoy doing, what you are passionate about, and where you have unique talents. They'll also help you identify what the needs are around you, which you may be able to fill—for extra income.

Don't be limited by what businesses already exist. Create your own unique business and make it work for you and your family! Do you love to cook? Market homemade freezer meals to two-income families who want to eat healthy and at home, but don't have the time or energy to do so. Do you enjoy baking? Offer homemade baked goods to those who love the taste of homemade, but simply don't have the time to bake bread, cookies or cakes themselves. Do you have a knack for decorating affordably? Market yourself as a decorator who comes in and uses what the customer already has to redecorate a room. Like to organize? Offer your services as a home or office organizer. In today's Internet age, it's never been easier to establish and market a home business.

Even Mark has supplemented our income with a side business. In the early ministry years, Mark was an independent flooring installer. This was his preministry job, and he has been able to do it on the side when needed. For several years, he had an eBay business with his friend Jeff. Together, Jeff and Mark would go to auctions, where they'd select items to purchase that they knew they could resell online. Because Jeff had more disposable income than we did, he would purchase the items, and then Mark would bring them home, post them on the Internet, and ship them out when they sold. Mark and Jeff split the profits. In recent years, Mark has served as a substitute carrier for a rural newspaper route. When he does the route, he always takes one of our kids with him to give them time to talk and to teach them a little bit about earning power.

With all of these home businesses, the best part is that Mark could decide when he wanted to work and when he didn't. If it was a busy season for the church or our family, the eBay business was placed on the back burner. If we had a lot on our schedule and he was asked to install carpet or substitute for the paper route, he simply said, "No, not this time." The income from these home businesses helped us build up our savings and pay off debt, but they also allowed us to keep our priority of family first.

LISTEN

Working together is a necessity for making a home business successful. When Jill was doing day care at home, she desperately needed a bit of "Jill" time each evening. It was during that season that Mark took on the responsibilities of bath and bedtime for our kids. They saw it as "daddy time." Jill saw it as some much-needed relief from the daily responsibilities of caring for children. When she taught piano and voice lessons in our home, Mark would prepare dinner on the nights she was teaching.

If you're going to embark upon some sort of a home business, discuss the realities of the time needed both at home and away from the home. Talk about your fears, your hopes and your dreams of what could be. Listen to one another's concerns and respond with empathy and a willingness to work together to find solutions to the challenges. If a financial investment needs to be made to launch the business, make sure you both agree on how and when that investment can be made.

ADJUST

When Jill taught piano and voice lessons in our home, Mark had to adjust to the fact that two days a week he would find non-family members in our living room when he arrived home from work. He knew that Jill was not only using her degree with her music business, but also that she was contributing to our income. Mark needed to adjust and help out in any way that he could to make it a win-win for all of us. Honestly, he looked at that time as specially reserved for him and our kids. While Jill was teaching, he would take the kids out in the yard or build Legos with them in the family room.

An adjustment Jill had to make was learning to set aside the time she needed to invest in the business. When the kids were young, she adjusted by using nap times to clean the kitchen, get Avon deliveries ready, or practice music for an upcoming wedding. She also had to learn to work in small chunks of time, because that's the reality of mixing home and business.

Introducing a home business can also add some stress to the family, so you want to make sure that a) you really need the income, and b) you really enjoy what you're doing. When we do something we love, it's a more natural fit for our family. When Jill was doing day care at home, it added some stress because being with that many kids all day wasn't her favorite thing to do. It wasn't the best fit for Jill or for us as a family. It was a logical solution to our situation and it served us well, but she just wouldn't have been able to do it longer than the two years that she did.

One final adjustment to consider: Set boundaries. When you go to work, boundaries are built into the workday. You have a designated time period for lunch. You have a set time when you go to work and leave. When you're working at home, you have to set those boundaries yourself. No one is going to do it for you. Identify when you will and when you will not work and stay true to your boundaries. Remember this is supposed to help, not hurt, your family.

NAVIGATE

If you decide to embark upon a home business, you'll need to market your skills. One of the best ways to do that is by word of mouth. When you begin, you can offer your services to friends and family at a discount. This can help create buzz and launch word-of-mouth marketing.

In this Internet age, you'll want to set up a Web site or blog to market your business and build a following. Think about what you have to offer the world and set up your Web site accordingly. If your business is a service you offer to others, establishing a blog can help create a following. For instance, if you are offering your services as an organizational consultant, you can blog about organizational topics that would be of interest to those struggling with organization. Tell others in your community about your blog, and make sure the address is on business cards you keep in your wallet or purse.

If you decide to pursue working out of your home, don't try to do it alone. Connect with others who are making a home business work. Online you'll find resources like Christian Work-at-Home Moms (cwahm.com) and Christian Work-at-Home Dads (cwahd.com). Mary Byer's blog (makingworkathomework.com) is another great resource.

If you are considering a home business, here are five Savvy Steps to being successful:

1. *Research.* Find out what others are making in the same business. If the service you are offering is completely unique, survey a test market to find out what people would realistically pay for a service like yours.

2. *Market.* Set up a Web site and/or a blog, create flyers, make phone calls, and do whatever else you need to do to get the word out. Sometimes simple word of mouth is the best marketing strategy. It might also pay to give away your services to a few choice people in exchange for their endorsements and the experience the job gives to you. Many photography businesses start out this way.

3. *Record.* Keep good records not only for tax purposes but also to maintain a careful eye on your income as well as expenses. If it's costing you more to run the business than you're making, it might not be the best business for you. (Keep in mind that many businesses

do have start-up costs at the very beginning.) Don't forget to keep meticulous records of business expenses so you can take the appropriate deductions on your taxes. Make sure and set aside 30 percent of your earnings for self-employment taxes too.

4. *Prioritize.* Remember, you're running a home business to help the family, not hurt the family. Keep your priorities in this order: God, self, spouse, children, business.

5. *Evaluate.* Don't be afraid to ask, "Is this working?" or "Is this profitable?" Discuss the pros and cons with your spouse to evaluate if this really is working well for your family.

It's important to note that part of being an entrepreneur is possibly dealing with failure. Even the most well-planned home business venture might not be as successful as you dream it will. It's important to keep this wisdom in mind from Crystal Paine, the author of the successful Money Saving Mom blog (moneysavingmom.com): "I've slowly learned over the past few years that failure of some kind is inevitable when you have your business or are trying to start working from home. Everything just isn't going to turn out exactly like you expected. In fact, much of the time, things will be a lot harder and a lot less successful than you planned or hoped or dreamed. Contrary to what I thought in the beginning, I've come to realize that failure is my friend. I've learned much more through failure than I have through success."[15]

Crystal tried many at-home business opportunities before she hit gold with her extremely popular blog. She is a perfect example of the adage, "If at first you don't succeed, try, try again." If you determine that some extra income would be helpful for the family and you're willing to learn from a failure or two, a home business

[15] www.moneysavingmom.com/money_saving_mom/2009/11/
becoming-a-workathome-mom-learning-through-failure-part-3.html

may be just the right thing for you. If you are a self-starter with some sense of self-discipline, you just might find that you can do something you love and get paid for it! Your goal is to have less time working and more time with the family. In some cases, a home business can provide just what you and your family need.

Lord, show us Your plan for income for our family. If we need to spend less, show us how. If we need to bring in more, give us wisdom to know how to turn our interests and passions into income. We need Your wisdom and Your creativity, God. Help us to have good conversations and set valuable direction for our family. In Jesus' name, amen.

let's talk about it

My thoughts after reading this chapter are ...

If we were to consider a home business, what options might we have?

What fears do you have about considering a home business?

chapter 18

are you a less-is-more family?

WE'RE GUESSING THAT BY THIS POINT YOU ARE ACTUALLY GLAD TO BE JUST ABOUT FINISHED READING THIS BOOK. It's not an easy book to digest, because it's challenging, thought-provoking and asks you to take real and often difficult action.

Truthfully, it wasn't an easy book for us to write for all the same reasons. We've committed to being a less-is-more family for many years, but there have been times when our vision has blurred, our faith has wavered, and our life has become too busy. During those times we've had to rethink, reorganize and recommit to what we really want for our family.

If you choose to join the less-is-more team, you'll find yourself needing to do the same on occasion. That's when you'll pull out the book again to read a few chapters and remind yourself of why you want to live with less. You'll need to refresh your vision of what "more" really looks like, and you'll probably also need to brush up on the attitudes and actions that will keep your family on track.

We've shared our story throughout the pages of this book. We've also shared the stories of other families who have decided to battle adult peer pressure in order to give their family the "mores" that are most important to them. Real stories give us real courage. To bolster your resolve and strengthen your determination, we'd like to share one more story with you. This is the story of the Leyden family, told in Peggy's own words, which she shared at a Hearts at Home Conference several years ago:

If you had told me five years ago that I would be a homeschooling stay-at-home mom with three children, I would have laughed at you and said you had the wrong woman. I was a senior manager at Arthur Andersen, prior to the Enron debacle, and believed I *had* to work at least close to full-time for us to manage our lives in Naperville, Illinois.

I am happy to tell you that God had different plans for our family! Shortly after Andersen fell apart due to the Enron scandal, I took another full-time role with a Chicago-based company doing change management and corporate training work. At this point we had two children and shortly thereafter, God blessed us with another healthy pregnancy, which was an unplanned blessing. I am so grateful for our little Rachel, because with her I really started to seriously evaluate our lives and listen to the increasing call on my heart to get home.

While pregnant with Rachel, I tried to arrange a part-time return to my job, but to no avail. I felt God saying, "Trust me and I will help you find a way." This was so scary because *I made three times what my husband did* and I wasn't sure how we were going to manage.

I started saving money as if they were going to stop printing it. I soon found myself at home with my children who were five, two, and a newborn. Using my networking skills, I kept in contact with all my old Andersen connections and other friends from the business world. I also wrote down all the types of training and work I could do—team development, leadership development, executive presentation skills, and so on.

Now life looks a lot different and the best part is that I am home most of the time! I do occasional part-time consulting projects and training, which allow me to keep my toes in the business world.

We've found that less is more. Yes, we are living on far less money. But we also have less stress. And what have we gained? More time, more availability and more faith. Our faith has grown as we have watched God provide for our family over and over. My encouragement to you is that God is faithful. He doesn't waste anything and He wants you to trust Him fully.

Jill recently talked with Peggy to find out how their family is still doing with this major transition. After stating that things were going well, she said, "You know, Jill, what I'm finding with my consulting is that I'm doing more of the work I love in less time." We love how she worded that! She's given up the big salary and the big title, but she still does what she loves occasionally while keeping her chosen priorities in the right place.

Not every family's transition to "family first" priorities is as drastic as the Leyden family's. Some of us are making smaller, but no less valuable, changes that help us redefine our priorities and put our family first. The question we have to ask ourselves is: Am I willing to stand up to the pressure of the world in order to give my family my best? Adult peer pressure is hard—maybe even harder than peer pressure in the teen years. But there is strength in numbers and we want you to know that you are not alone in this journey.

It was G. K. Chesterton who said, "There are two ways to get enough: One is to continue to accumulate more and more. The other is to desire less." Families like Peggy's are desiring less so that their family can have enough. Our hope is that you will join us on the less-is-more journey. We're living life differently, and loving the benefits.

If you began this process and this book not yet convinced, we hope we've broadened your perspective. If you were already living with less, we hope we've strengthened your commitment. More than anything, our prayer is that we've all been reminded of the attitudes and the actions it takes to keep our heads, hearts and bodies at home as much as possible. That's the "more" that every family needs.

"For I know the plans I have for you," declares the LORD, "plans to prosper you and not to harm you, plans to give you hope and a future. Then you will call upon me and come and pray to me, and I will listen to you. You will seek me and find me when you seek me with all your heart."
Jeremiah 29:11–13 (NIV)

Dear Readers,

Have you decided to be a less-is-more family? We'd love to hear how this book has encouraged you personally! You can e-mail Jill at jillannsavage@yahoo.com and Mark at jamsavage7@yahoo.com.

You'll also find more encouragement on the less-is-more concept on our Web sites and blogs.

> Jill's blog and Web site: www.jillsavage.org
> Mark's blog: www.dadyoucandoit.blogspot.com
> Hearts at Home blog and Web site: www.hearts-at-home.org

> Joining you on the journey,
> *Jill and Mark Savage*

The Hearts at Home organization is committed to meeting the needs of moms. Founded in 1993, Hearts at Home offers a variety of resources and events to assist women in their jobs as wives and mothers.

In addition to this book, our resources include the Heartbeat radio program and our extensive Hearts at Home Web site. Additionally, Hearts at Home events make a great getaway for individuals, moms' groups, or for that special friend, sister or sister-in-law. The regional conferences, attended by more than ten thousand women each year, provide a unique, affordable and highly encouraging weekend for any mom in any season of motherhood.

Hearts at Home, 1509 N. Clinton Blvd., Bloomington, Illinois 61702
(309) 828-MOMS
hearts@hearts-at-home.org
www.hearts-at-home.org